DROPPING the GLOVES

BARRY MELROSE

WITH ROGER VAUGHAN

DROPPING

INSIDE THE FIERCELY COMBATIVE

the GLOVES

WORLD OF PROFESSIONAL HOCKEY

WITH A FOREWORD BY WAYNE GRETZKY

FENN
M&S

Library and Archives Canada Cataloguing in Publication

Melrose, Barry
   Dropping the gloves / Barry Melrose.

ISBN 978-0-7710-5694-9

   1. Hockey players--Biography. 2. National Hockey
League--Biography. I. Title.

GV848.5.A1M44 2012   796.962092'2   C2012-900974-1

We acknowledge the financial support of the Government of Canada through the
Canada Book Fund and that of the Government of Ontario through the Ontario
Media Development Corporation's Ontario Book Initiative. We further acknowledge
the support of the Canada Council for the Arts and the Ontario Arts Council for our
publishing program.

Published simultaneously in the United States of America by McClelland & Stewart,
a division of Random House of Canada Limited
P.O. Box 1030, Plattsburgh, New York 12901

Library of Congress Control Number: 2012932353

Typeset in Bembo by M&S, Toronto
Printed and bound in the United States of America

McClelland & Stewart, a division of Random House of Canada Limited
Suite 300
One Toronto Street,
Toronto, Ontario
M5C 2V6
www.mcclelland.com

1   2   3   4   5   16   15   14   13   12

For Cindy and my two sons, Tyrell and Adrien

Thanks to everyone I ever played with,
and to everyone who played for me.

— B.M.

For Kippy

Thanks to Kristina Pereira Tully, Tom Baker,
Mary P. Vogel, Hannah Blackwood, Jeff Fellows,
Michael Melgaard, and Jim Fitzgerald.

— R.V.

Contents

Foreword

by WAYNE GRETZKY

I'm glad Barry Melrose has done this book because not only does he really understand the game of hockey, no one talks about it better than Barry. He's passionate about it. Anyone who has seen him on TV knows this. I had the privilege of listening to him in the dressing room and on the bench, up close and personal. That was even better.

Barry is one of the best coaches I ever played for. His idea of how the game should be played focused on speed – speed that would highlight the talents of the skilled players. I was in total agreement with that. He and I had a meeting of the minds on day one. From then on, it was a pleasure playing for him. Sometimes it was an adventure, because Barry was always willing to try things. He never got on a guy's case for being aggressively creative. That was lucky for me.

As a coach, Barry treated every player on the team as an individual. He made it a point to know each guy inside and out. He knew what each of them could do, what motivated them, and when to use them in the best possible way. As a player, you really can't ask for more than that.

As a TV presenter, Barry brings great insight and good humour to our game. In *Dropping the Gloves*, he takes you behind the scenes in junior hockey, the American Hockey League, and the NHL, as player and coach.

Barry and I are about the same age (actually, he's a few years older!). I'm from a small town in Canada myself, and went through the same progression he did as a player. When I read this book, I had to chuckle, because he really got it right: the tough times, the good times, the wild and crazy stuff – it's all here. And I totally agree with his conclusion that our game is in great shape.

After reading this book, you'll find yourself watching hockey more intently, and with a deeper appreciation of what's going on out there on the ice.

Nice job, guys.

Wayne Gretzky
LOS ANGELES, 2012

Introduction

There Is No Ball In Hockey

Hockey has little in common with the other four professional sports in North America. Unlike base*ball*, foot*ball*, basket*ball*, and soccer – called foot*ball* everywhere else in the world – there is no *ball* in hockey. Unless you are a kid growing up in the frozen north, or directed into the sport at a very early age by relatives or close friends, you will not choose to play on the ice with a hard rubber disk that can easily break a bone or knock out teeth instead of on the ground with a round, much friendlier ball.

Hockey players who make the professional leagues get started early. They must make a strong commitment to the game and its traditions well before they are teenagers, making it their primary life focus until they retire. Hockey is more than a game. It is a way of life.

Barry Melrose's hockey career is typical. Barry grew up in a small town in Saskatchewan, Canada, started skating as soon as he could walk, took his first stick to the face at age five, went through the Canadian junior hockey system, played eight years in the NHL, and coached at all levels before joining ESPN as the most knowledgeable and interesting analyst of the game.

I first met Barry at ESPN in the 1990s when I was working on a pre-Olympic program. It was a warm, summer day. Here came this big, friendly looking guy walking through the lobby in shorts and a polo shirt, wearing flip-flops, his hair in a mullet, with people greeting him, "Hey coach." I got to know Barry.

During the 2011 NHL playoffs, I found myself astonished by the elevated quality of play I was seeing: the crisp passing, the 100-mile-an-hour shots, the size and speed of the players, the solid hits and brilliant plays, the extraordinary goaltending – the overall frenetic pace of the game. Right then, it occurred to me that taking a close look inside this game would be both fascinating and illuminating. I called Barry because I couldn't think of anyone who loves the game more, who knows more about the game, and who can talk about it as eloquently. Barry Melrose is a triple threat – the consummate hockey guy. Proof of that is in this book.

Enjoy.

Roger Vaughan
OXFORD, MARYLAND

Warriors on Ice

Hockey is a great chess match played on sharp steel blades on a sheet of ice 200 by 85 feet surrounded by a solid wall (the boards) four feet high. It's a game played by guys moving at thirty miles an hour with a round, hard rubber puck three inches in diameter by one inch thick that weighs six ounces and travels between ninety and 105 miles an hour when launched by a skilled player with a composite stick that flexes like a bow firing an arrow.

Hockey's origins can be traced back to pre-Christian era stick-and-ball games adapted for icy conditions. Among the early "hockey players" were the First Nation Mi'kmaq of eastern Canada. There are indications that the game they played on ice included the harsh, physical aspects of other Mi'kmaq sports, namely lacrosse. The result was a hard-hitting, violent contest, and that concept is still the backbone of today's professional game of hockey.

Lacrosse was invented by First Nation tribes as a way of training warriors. There's a lot of lacrosse in hockey. Lacrosse is played on foot with sticks that have a head strung with netting to catch, cradle, pass, and shoot a hard rubber ball about the size of a tennis ball into a small (six-foot) square goal. Players wear shorts, minimal pads, protective gloves, and helmets. It's a full-contact game, one of the fastest team sports played on foot. There are ten men on a team – including a goalie – instead of the six players on a hockey team. Lacrosse combines tough, physical play with finesse, making it the dry-land version of hockey – or vice versa, since lacrosse came first. Many of the great hockey players, including Wayne Gretzky, Brendan Shanahan, Joe Sakic, and Paul Kariya, played lacrosse during the off-season while growing up.

I always compare hockey players to warriors, because First Nation history lays down a tradition that Canadian kids still embrace. Kids love the idea of being warriors, especially when the tradition is in their nation's blood, and when every winter the ice on the ponds makes the best playgrounds.

1

Ice: The Best Playground

I can't remember life without hockey. My dad built a rink when I was really young, maybe three or four years old. I remember him making a twenty-foot-square enclosure with two-by-six planks and packing it with snow. What made it a difficult job was the fact we didn't have running water on the farm. When he built the rink, we had an artesian well pumped by a windmill. We had a big trough for watering the cattle. In the winter you had to keep a fire going under it so ice wouldn't form in the below-zero temperatures. He'd put three 100-gallon barrels on a sled and fill them with buckets from the trough. Then he'd pull the sled to the rink and bucket the water out of the barrels. It would take two or three trips to make a good ice surface. My mother would help me into my skates, and I'd walk out the kitchen door onto the rink. When I got older, I realized how much work it was for my dad to build that rink.

I remember the whole family being out there. I can barely recall skating on it, but I can picture the rink. Another really early memory was being at the arena in my hometown, Kelvington, Saskatchewan. That's five hundred miles north of the U.S. border at western North Dakota – and four hundred miles northwest of Winnipeg, Manitoba. I remember my dad taking me in there and putting me on the ice. I fell on my head. I was four or five. In those days we didn't wear helmets. I went out there and fell on my head. It wasn't a very auspicious start to my career.

I was five years old at my first hockey practice. I was hit in the face with a stick and got a big black eye. I had a little leather helmet on, but one of the other kids spun around and his stick got me. I started bawling, and my dad came out. He was mad because I was bawling. He was telling me to shut up. My eye blackened and closed, so at least he could see that I wasn't just being a wimp – the stick actually did some damage. I don't think my grandfather and my dad figured they had a budding NHL player on their hands.

Kelvington, where I grew up, is a typical Saskatchewan town of about nine hundred people. Most people there farmed, growing wheat. Nowadays in Saskatchewan canola is probably the biggest crop. But in the old days it was cereal grains – wheat, barley, and oats.

Every town in Saskatchewan has three things: a legion hall, a skating rink, and a curling rink. I remember watching my mom and dad curl, and then spending the rest of my time in the skating rink. We also had a movie theatre and two Chinese restaurants. When I was really little, the town had two hotels, which meant there were also two bars. But then the one hotel closed, leaving us with only one hotel and one bar. The population of almost a thousand people made it a big town for Saskatchewan, a big small town.

Everything up there depended on how far you could haul grain. If you were closer to Wadena than Kelvington, you took your grain to Wadena. We got farm produce from a radius of twenty miles. All the sizable towns had grain elevators. If you look at pictures of western Canada, you'll see these tall structures in the middle of the flatlands. The number of grain elevators in town determined how wealthy an area you were, because the more grain you produced, the more elevators you had. Kelvington was a five-elevator town, which was pretty good.

Winter was tough and started early. I can remember one time we had snow for Halloween. One year, we had snow every month except July. We had a big snowstorm one June – I woke up one morning and there was six inches of snow on the ground. We also had a snowstorm at the end of August that year. That was very rare, but it shows you how bad the weather could be. Winters were always long. They were also really cold. Everyone had block heaters in their cars. When you went to bed at night, you plugged in your car, and the little heater kept your oil from freezing. My dad used to cut out a piece of cardboard and put it in front of the radiator. He'd cut a hole in the middle of the cardboard to let a little air through. The cardboard would keep the heat in, and prevent too much cold air from getting to the radiator. That made the water and oil warm up faster, so you'd get heat sooner.

I've got two sisters. My older sister, Vicky, was a schoolteacher in Saskatchewan her whole life. She retired in 2011. I have a younger sister, Cindy, who married a farmer in Kelvington. I have a younger brother, Warren, who also stayed in Kelvington. He runs a pig farm.

My father was a third-generation farmer. My great-grandfather and grandfather came over from Scotland in the 1920s and started farming in Saskatchewan. My dad followed in their footsteps. And then I came along. The plan was for me to be the fourth generation, unless I could figure out something else to do, like making a career in hockey.

I realize I had a great time growing up. It was awesome. Growing up on a farm meant you had to work, but I know it was good for me. My parents and my grandparents were sports fans, and I was a big, athletic kid, so I played all sports. My dad coached my hockey and baseball teams. I spent a lot of time with my family because of that, going to tournaments and games. I was very fortunate. I had a great set of parents, a great set of grandparents. Kelvington was a super place to grow up.

Because Kelvington was so isolated, sports were very important. There weren't a whole lot of other things for kids to do. My parents never once said no to me about playing a sport. I played football in high school, and I played basketball and volleyball. Obviously, hockey was the big sport. From an early age I knew I was going to play hockey. Hockey is so big in Canada, so important. Every little town has a pee wee team – Rose Valley, Wadena, Quill Lake, Foam Lake, Watson. You start playing against the kids you go to school with when you are five or six. If you stay around, you play against them for the rest of your life. In Canada, hockey is so much more serious, so much more competitive than other sports.

Lacrosse may be Canada's national sport – many people don't know that, even Canadians – but Canadians are most passionate about hockey. They are nuts about hockey, fanatic about their home teams the way people in Green Bay are crazy about the Packers. Season tickets in Montreal and Toronto are handed down through the generations.

As a kid, I loved history. I'd read hockey's history, the history of the NHL, the history of the Toronto Maple Leafs and of all six original NHL teams. I knew Montreal was originally called Ville-Marie, and that its present name comes from Mount Royal, a hill with three peaks in the middle of the city. I immersed myself in hockey lore. I knew all the big names who had played hockey over the years, guys like Red Kelly, George Armstrong, Bobby Baun, Bill Gadsby, Pierre Pilote, and Dave Keon.

My wildest dreams wouldn't have included meeting those guys that were like gods to me growing up, but I ended up meeting most of them. I played against Keon once, when he was at the end of his great career. It was in Hartford, Connecticut. After the game we were in a bar, and a teammate took me over and introduced me to him. I said hello and told him I loved how he played, and then I just sat there not saying a word in this bar in Hartford, listening to these guys talk and thinking to myself, "I am having a beer with Davey Keon."

I knew that Lord Stanley of Preston – Frederick Arthur Stanley – had been appointed Governor General of Canada by Queen Victoria in 1888. I knew how he had gotten so crazy about hockey that he donated a cup to be awarded annually to Canada's top-ranking amateur hockey club. I knew it was won for the first time in 1893 by the Montreal Hockey Club. Today we know it as the Stanley Cup.

I also played baseball growing up. Combined, the two sports took up a lot of my time. I went from hockey season to baseball season. A couple of weeks waiting for the baseball diamonds to dry up, or a couple of weeks waiting for the village freeze — those periods were my only off-seasons.

In baseball, I was a catcher. I was probably better at baseball than I was at hockey. I was both a good hitter and a good catcher. I even had scouts looking at me. A lot of people around Kelvington still say I was a better baseball player than hockey player.

A kid I played against, Terry Puhl, went on to a baseball career. He played with the Houston Astros for fifteen years. But I never once thought of baseball as a possible career. I just played it because the rinks weren't frozen. I really loved hockey — the skating, the contact. I loved everything about the game. It was the perfect sport for me. That was really where my passion was. I liked baseball, too, and I enjoyed playing all sports, but hockey was the sport I was really drawn to.

I grew up with guys who were the best baseball players in the province, and the best football players — guys who went on to play pro football for the Saskatchewan Roughriders. But that wasn't the same as being the best hockey player in town, or in the province. Hockey was held at a whole other level.

In Canada, a small town's rink is its social centre. Everyone gathers there. The kids went to the skating rink, the adults went to the curling rink. Every night you'd skate there for a couple of hours with your friends. The senior hockey team in a small town is very important, and Kelvington had a good one. My friend Wendel Clark's father, Les, was their coach, and that team was like a semi-pro team. As a little kid, all you wanted to do was play for the pee wee league teams — and you dreamed of going on to play senior hockey. Pee wee was made up of kids aged ten to twelve. There would be fifteen hundred fans at pee wee games, the rink would be packed. So that was always my early goal, to play for a pee wee team.

I was lucky to be in Kelvington. By the time I was growing up, we had indoor rinks, an indoor curling rink and an indoor hockey rink. Actually, most towns had indoor rinks when I was a young kid. Canada's Centennial, a year-long celebration of the Canadian Confederation, happened in 1967. Every town or village had a Centennial project. A lot of towns in Saskatchewan built an arena, which is why you see so many indoor rinks with names like Porcupine Centennial Arena, Quill Lake Centennial Arena. In Kelvington, we already had a good arena, so we built a great golf course, which is still in use today.

Porcupine, Quill Lake – all these small towns produced NHL players. A lot of good athletes came out of there during the seventies. I was a farmer, Joey Kocur was a farmer. Wendel Clark, Kerry Clark, Kory Kocur (Joey's cousin) – all those guys came out of Kelvington. Out at Quill Lake, thirty miles away, were the Odelein brothers, Selmar and Lyle. At Foam Lake, which was sixty miles away, were Dennis Polonich and Bernie Federko. At Hudson Bay, a hundred miles away, was Trent Yawney. And Kelly Chase came out of Porcupine. There were ten of us from that small area who made it to the NHL.

Bernie Federko and I played together all the way up. As a kid, I played for Foam Lake in some tournaments, and Bernie played for Kelvington. Foam Lake won the provincial championship when Bernie played for them. He won the league scoring title one year as a bantam player. He would go on to have a great junior career with the Saskatoon Blades, setting a team record for assists that still stands. Then he played fourteen seasons in the NHL, mostly for St. Louis. He was elected into the Hockey Hall of Fame.

These guys are all around my age. Dennis Polonich is older than me, but other than that it goes Dennis, me, Bernie, Trent, Wendel, Joey, then Kelly, then the Odelein brothers. We're all within a few years of each other. When I had my hockey school, they all were teachers.

It's surprising that so many quality players came from such a small area. It's a unique place in Saskatchewan – in all of Canada for that matter. If you look at the common denominators, you'll find we were all basically raised the same way. The majority of us were farmers. We all came from great homes, with great parents. We were taught a strong work ethic by our parents. And our parents were committed to promoting our careers.

If parents aren't involved, it's virtually impossible for a kid to play hockey. Number one, it costs a lot. Number two, there's tons of travel. So if your mom and dad aren't willing or able to pay the costs and take you places, it's really tough to play. That's true in all sports, but more so in hockey because of the cost of ice time. You're not paying to use a high school gym for basketball, you're not paying to use a field outside for soccer or football or baseball. But if you're playing hockey, you're paying to use that ice. And it's expensive – it can be up to two hundred and fifty dollars an hour these days.

The equipment is also expensive, but it's the skates that really hammer you. Today, a good pair of skates – not even a great pair – costs four hundred dollars. And, when you're a kid, skates only last a year because your feet grow so fast. On top of that, the new composite sticks are two or three hundred dollars each.

When I was growing up, there were skates called Tackaberry, made by CCM. "Tacks" we called them — the greatest skates in the world. All the NHL players wore them, so all the kids wanted them, myself included. I had to earn my pair.

My dad gave me a piglet for working on the farm. I let that pig grow, raised it up. It eventually had piglets of its own. I sold four of the pigs when they got to be two hundred pounds. When you sold a grown pig in those days, you'd usually get sixty or seventy dollars. But of course, I sold mine during a dip in the market. Instead of getting sixty or seventy dollars a pig, I got twenty. That's a good indication of my farming capabilities. A pair of Tackaberrys cost sixty-seven dollars at the time, so it took all four pigs to get me that first pair. I was fourteen. I wore them for one year. They were made out of kangaroo leather. Of course, kangaroos are protected now — you can't get kangaroo leather — but they were just unbelievable skates. I'll always remember the day they arrived in the mail. When you're fifty-five and you still remember something like that, it indicates what an impact it had on your life.

I played outdoors to begin with. Kelvington has Prouse Lake, which is really a little pond. We would skate on the lake for a few weeks early in the season until the ice in the rink was ready. The early skates I had were terrible — my ankles would turn over all the time at first. When my sons were young, I got them some really good skates, and they never had that problem. If there had been skates like we have today when I was a kid, I would have been a much better skater early on. But at first I was out there on the ice with my ankles turned over, wobbling around. Like I said, I don't think my dad thought he had an NHL player on his hands when he first saw me skating. But I was a big, strong kid, and my ankles adjusted pretty fast.

We kids had to help maintain the ice. There were no Zambonis. We used a fifty-gallon barrel of boiling water on wheels, with a network of tubing that came off the top, ran down the back of the barrel, and spread out about six feet across the ice with rags hanging off it. The bottom tube had holes every couple of inches where the water dribbled out and wet the rags. You pulled the barrel at a steady pace, going around the rink, with the water coming out and flooding the ice in strips. It took about three barrels to restore the ice to a nice smooth sheet. We'd do it on skates so we wouldn't leave footprints. At the end of the night, the last thing you did after public skating or hockey was scrape the ice really well, then flood it with the barrels. After you finished, you'd turn out the lights, lock the doors, and go home.

In my early years we had house leagues where you divided up all the kids by age groups. Kids' leagues were divided into four teams that would play against each other. You'd have a travel team that would play games against other towns, but the majority of the games were played in this house league.

I remember playing one away game in the Tiny Tims when I was five. We went to Preeceville, and it was really scary for me to go onto a different ice surface in a different town. In Kelvington, I knew everyone, so it seemed weird to play with strangers. We only played the one away game that year, and I was glad of that.

Things have changed, but when I was growing up the kids eight and under were called Tiny Tims, ten and under were Tom Thumbs, twelve and under were pee wees, fourteen and under were bantams, sixteen and under were midgets.

Today kid's hockey is very organized, with a lot of new leagues for different age groups. Hockey Canada, the main governing body of the sport, has divided the minor league players into mini mites (ages one and two), mites (three and four), tykes (five and six), novices (seven and eight), atoms (nine and ten), pee wees (eleven and twelve), bantams (thirteen and fourteen), midgets (fifteen through seventeen), and juveniles (eighteen to twenty).

Les Clark, my friend Wendel's dad – Wendel is also my second cousin – was one of the first guys who coached me. He ran the Kelvington arena and the senior team. And there was a teacher named Ken Vanos who started the house league system in Kelvington. He also coached me when I was in pee wee. Mr. Clark and Mr. Vanos were probably the two guys who had the most influence on my play as a kid. And of course my father and grandfather, because they had to drive me everywhere.

My dad never played hockey. He had to quit school in Grade 8 and go to work on the farm. But both he and my grandfather loved sports, so I always had lots of pushing from them, lots of support. They always got me where I needed to go. But on the ice, the two people I talked to in Kelvington were Mr. Clark and Mr. Vanos.

There was no formal introduction to the game. You just started playing, that's the way it was. You were put onto a team and there wasn't a lot of instruction. It was nothing like it is today, with all the kids going to hockey school. I didn't go to hockey school until I was fourteen. It wasn't as if you had power skating instruction and four hours a day of coaching. You were just divided into teams and told to play.

I picked up a lot of stuff by listening and watching. I read a lot of books. I used to watch the seniors practise all the time, and I'd hear Les Clark yelling, "You've got to learn to stop both ways!" When you're just free skating for fun, you always skate one way, and that causes you to learn to do things one way. You'd be surprised how many senior kids couldn't stop both ways when they needed to change directions. I was a sponge. I read every book I could get my hands on, especially books written by guys from the NHL. I read Gordie Howe's book, and Bobby Hull's. At public skating, I would try and make the moves those guys made.

We had TV, but there was only two channels. The best sports show on TV was *Hockey Night in Canada* on Saturday nights. It's still on today. I'd get my chores done, get the popcorn made, and I'd be in front of the TV for *Hockey Night*. The games always started in progress, at the ten-minute mark of the first period. I never got to see a full game until I got older. It was always Toronto or Montreal. Just like the kids after me who watched Wayne Gretzky, or now Sidney Crosby, when I saw guys do something on the ice, I couldn't wait to try it. I was a defenceman so I was always watching Tim Horton, my favourite, and always trying to do the things he did. When he was interviewed, I'd be hanging on every word.

It's funny, because I ended up playing for Toronto, and Ronny Ellis was one of my teammates there. Ronny was on those Maple Leafs teams I had watched as a little kid, so when

I got to Toronto I really enjoyed talking to him about all that stuff I couldn't get enough of during that one game a week I could see. We didn't have cable networks or anything like that, so *Hockey Night in Canada* was it until I got a lot older.

The TV set was black and white, with a nineteen-inch screen, and you thought it was magic. You didn't think you were smart enough to even touch it, let alone turn it on or off, but on Saturday night I never missed *Hockey Night in Canada.*

That was the extent of the professional sports I saw. Sunday nights, my grandfather and I would also always watch Red Skelton, and then *Bonanza.* That was the Sunday night TV selection.

In the summer, there would be one baseball game broadcast a week. I grew up cheering for the Yankees. They were often the game of the week because they were so good. In the fall, you'd have one football game a week. I was a Green Bay Packers fan for the same reason, and they weren't that far away in Wisconsin. That was the 1960s. Green Bay was always on TV because they were the best team. I still cheer for them today.

Bobby Orr came into the NHL in the late '60s. I loved the way he played. I wanted to play like him. He always seemed to have the puck. In a small town, you didn't always have enough players, so by playing defence I was able to play more of the game – twenty-five to twenty-eight minutes as opposed to the twenty minutes a forward might play. I'd want to be out on the ice, always having the puck like Bobby Orr. Plus, I was a big kid, stocky, and probably not fast enough to play on the red line.

I remember I used to go to the rink when it was open for public skating every night to try stuff, learning to stop and turn both ways. By then, my dad was running the rink, so I was on the ice all day every weekend. The old saying is, "Practise the things you can't do." I took that to heart. I was never able to turn to my right as easily as I could to my left, so I was always practising turning to my right. It was the same with stopping. I was much better stopping to my left, so I always worked on stopping to my right. If I'd had a dollar for every time I went public skating, I'd probably have been a wealthy kid.

I was determined to be a hockey player. Not everyone thought that made much sense. In Grade 9, our science teacher, Mr. Harrison, handed out a questionnaire. He told us to fill it out, and at the bottom we were supposed to write five lines about what we were going to do when we got out of high school – what we were going to do when we became adults, in other words. I wrote that I was going to play junior hockey, and then I was going to get drafted and play in the NHL. A couple of days later, Mr. Harrison called me into his office and he said, "Barry, I read your questionnaire. It was very well done, very thoughtful. This stuff about the NHL, it's fun, but seriously, what are you going to do when you're through with school – are you going to university, are you going to be a farmer like your dad? What are you going to be?" And I said, "Mr. Harrison, I'm going to play in the NHL." And he said, "Okay, okay, Barry. That's good, Barry," and he let me go with that tone that says, "Lots of luck, kid."

At that time, there were really no examples of anyone from Kelvington having a career in the NHL. Lloyd Gronsdahl had played a few games for Boston in the '50s. He was it. So there wasn't exactly a beaten path from little Kelvington to the big leagues.

A buddy of mine, Darryl Gillings, who's now a dentist, had an aunt who lived in Flin Flon, a big junior hockey town. Bobby Clarke had played there, Reggie Leach had played there. It's one of the most famous hockey towns in Canada. The Flin Flon Bombers are the junior team. Flin Flon is a mining town named after a character, Flintabattey Flonatin, from a novel by the name of *The Sunless City*. There's a big statue of Flintabattey on the outskirts of Flin Flon. In the book, Flintabattey pilots a submarine through a hole lined with gold in a bottomless lake and passes through into a strange, underground world. Today, I think about that story and shake my head, but to us kids back then, it was just the way it was.

When I was maybe thirteen and Darryl was fourteen, he and I went to a hockey school in Flin Flon. It was the only hockey school I ever attended. They had NHL guys there. They also had Flin Flon Bomber players there as instructors. I was there six days, Monday to Saturday, and it was awesome. I was five foot five, 150 pounds, heavy and big for my age, but I was one of the younger kids there. I started really growing when I was fifteen – I went from five foot seven to six foot one in one year. But even when I was only thirteen, I was still one of the bigger kids.

We started doing fundamentals at this school, and I thought that was crazy. "What am I doing with these older guys? It's not fair." But looking back, it's the best thing that ever happened to me, because I had to work harder than everyone else or I would have been creamed, outskated, or both. It turned out to be a blessing in disguise.

At the end of every hockey school, there's a reward in the form of a game. I was playing with those older kids, but I didn't feel out of place. I handled the puck a lot that night and was really happy with the way I played.

The Flin Flon rink was tiny. It's still there; they've never built a new one. It's called the Whitney Forum. When you are thirteen, everything looks big to you. I went back and played there when I was seventeen, in junior hockey, and I couldn't believe how much the building had shrunk.

It's crowded when there are ten guys on the ice of a small arena, but it made me keep my head up. You *had* to play with your head up. We wore helmets, but not face masks. If you didn't have your head up, you'd get banged. No more looking at the puck. If you did that, you were going to be laid out on your back real quick.

It's funny, but that has changed thanks to more effective helmets, face masks, and generally better equipment. These days, the kids are padded so well they can't get hurt easily. So they skate with their heads down. Players going through the system get used to that, and as a result, you see a lot more players skating with their heads down. Of course, you can also go faster that way. That's why you see so many big hits now, because guys carrying the puck are flying around with their heads down.

When I was starting out, there was hitting all over the place. There were no rules against hitting from behind. You started playing hockey when you were five, and that's when you started checking each other. Today, bodychecking isn't allowed until the kids are at least twelve.

At the end of the Flin Flon hockey school, the instructors brought each of us in to have a talk. A guy named Mel Pearson, who had played in the NHL, spoke with me. He said, "Barry, I think you're going to play in the NHL someday." I left that room flying. It was one of those amazing moments when someone gives you a pat on the back at just the right time, reinforcement that what you're doing is working. I'll remember that for the rest of my life.

2

The Only Game In Town

The man who launched me toward the NHL was Dwight McMillan. Dwight was the coach of the Weyburn Red Wings, a junior hockey team in southern Saskatchewan, a four-hour drive from Kelvington.

Wadena, Kelvington's most hated rival, was going to this really tough tournament in Assiniboia, Saskatchewan. I was fifteen, playing midget hockey, and they asked me to play with them. That's where I got scouted by Dwight. He was a new coach at the time, and would end up winning more games than any other junior coach in Canada. He was looking out for new players, and I impressed him at this tournament.

Dwight came looking for me, but he was looking for a kid he thought was from Wadena. He was driving around the wrong town looking for me. He finally went into a café and asked if anybody knew where Barry Melrose lived. They told him the only Melroses they knew lived in Kelvington. Dwight drove up and found me.

Dwight got me to come to Weyburn for summer hockey camp. All the junior hockey teams run summer camps for their regular players and to take a closer look at new kids like me. Camp lasted four days. When my dad came to pick me up, I told him Dwight wanted to speak with him. Dwight was talking with all the parents, so I thought he would just say, "Barry did a good job. Thank you very much for coming." My dad talked with Dwight, and he came out looking kind of blank. I was worried a little, so I asked him, "What did Dwight say? What do I need to work on?" And my dad said he wanted me to come to Weyburn and start school in two weeks. I just about fell off the chair. I'll always remember that talk with my dad. It's one thing to really want something, and quite another when it is there, staring you in the face. But my dad was a practical man, always calm in the face of calamity. He took things one at a time. We went home and told my mom. She wasn't quite as calm as my dad. But two weeks later, I was in Weyburn, starting school.

That was scary. My dad and grandfather drove me down there the day before school started. They got me situated with my billets, the people I would stay with, and I'll always remember how I felt watching my dad and grandfather drive away. That moment was the lowest point in my life.

I was doing what I wanted to do, but I'd never travelled before. For me, spending a night at a buddy's was a big deal. I'd stayed overnight a few times at players' houses when we'd had away games, but I always knew my dad was just down the road at a hotel. When my dad and granddad drove away that night in Weyburn, it was like a movie. There I was, at the window of my room, in this strange house with a family I didn't know, watching their car pull away. I watched the taillights to the end of the street, then the car turned and the lights disappeared. That was the hardest thing I've ever been through.

That first week at school was disorienting. It was all new kids, of course, and in Weyburn they were on the semester system, which I'd never even heard of before. In Kelvington, you had your own homeroom, and the teachers came to you. In Weyburn, you had to go to different rooms for every subject. I was late for classes because I couldn't find my classrooms. The school was gigantic. It felt more like a university. We had lockers, and I'd never had a locker before. I felt like a real country hick. I was a pretty lonely, confused boy for a while.

Once I figured it all out, school wasn't too hard for me. I was lucky to be a very good student. But it took me a while to catch up. The four classes I took in the first semester were beyond where I was in those subjects. But I had good fundamentals. I had no trouble with school once I caught up.

Today, all the junior hockey teams have tutors, and it's a good system. But when I was playing, the majority of the guys didn't get through Grade 12. I graduated because my parents demanded it. They valued education. The principal in Weyburn was a help to me. I had missed too many classes in one subject. He would have kicked most guys out, but he called me in. He said he knew I was passing the subject, but he told me not to miss another class. So I didn't. But most guys didn't care, and when they quit school and took jobs so they'd have more money, the team didn't care either.

I remember thinking Weyburn was gigantic. It was a city

of ten thousand people. I'd never seen anything like it before. I thought it was like Chicago or New York.

Here's a story that will show you what a hick I was. My buddy, Darryl Gillings, got married young. He was seventeen and his girlfriend was fifteen. At fifteen, I was his best man. My girlfriend and I drove to Yorkton with Darryl and his fiancée, Darlene, to get their wedding rings. That was right after I'd been to camp in Weyburn. Yorkton was a town of around fifteen thousand people, a big city to me. We parked on the outskirts of town and walked all the way to the mall because we weren't comfortable driving where there were traffic lights at intersections. It was a long walk. I'd driven farm machinery since I was twelve years old, cars and trucks on the road since I was thirteen, but never with traffic lights.

In 2012, Kelvington still doesn't have traffic lights. None of the small towns in Saskatchewan do. I remember when I took my test for my driver's licence in Kelvington, we couldn't find two cars together on the street so that I could parallel park. So I parallel parked behind one car.

Junior hockey is a business. In Weyburn, the city owned the team. Other towns had private ownership. In either case, it's run as a business: the coach is paid, all the employees are paid. They sell advertising in the program, and they sell tickets. If it was a city-owned team, they were in it to at least break even. If it was a privately owned team, they were in it to make money.

The teams become the identity of those small towns in the Prairies. In most cases, junior hockey is the only game in town, and it's a great bang for the buck. The Weyburn Red Wings and the Estevan Bruins are famous teams because they have been around for so long. They have one of the great rivalries in junior hockey. The two towns are only an hour-and-a-half drive apart, and they hate each other. It only took one game for me to hate Estevan. I still hate it today. It's like the hatred between Kelvington and Wadena. I was raised hating Wadena. Those are rivalries like Toronto and Montreal. Those two NHL teams often met in the playoffs during the 1950s and 1960s, and every time the rivalry got stronger.

In the old days, the NHL owned many junior teams, which is why the teams often had the nicknames, like Red Wings and Bruins, of their parent clubs. If an NHL team saw a kid's potential when he was thirteen years old, it could put him on its "protected" list. That team would own his rights for the rest of his life, or until it traded him. I think Bobby Orr was owned by the Bruins when he was thirteen, although he didn't start playing in their farm system until he was fourteen. If Detroit found good young players from Saskatchewan, they sent them to Weyburn.

Cities took over and started running the teams on their own in the 1960s. In addition to Weyburn, the Red Wings sponsored junior teams in provinces all across Canada. It became too expensive to maintain that system, and when expansion happened in 1967 and six teams were added to the NHL, the amateur draft came in. The days of the old farm systems were gone for good.

You can get into junior hockey without being scouted, but it's rare. Every team has a system of paid scouts, as well as bird dogs, volunteers who get fringe benefits. They can be very effective because they know the game and they take pride in being involved in it.

Bird dogs are old hockey guys, many of them former players and coaches, who love hanging out at the old rinks around the country. They were minor celebrities in western Canada. Everyone knew them, bought them coffee. Wearing their team jackets and hats, they'd go to games all over the place, looking for talented young players. They had their travel paid for, and when they did find a kid, they got bragging rights for life if the player turned out to be good. The best bird dogs ended up as paid scouts.

Many of these guys were Royal Canadian Mounted Police. A lot of the smaller Canadian towns have three or four Mounties assigned to it. A lot of them coached kids' hockey, baseball, and lacrosse. When I was growing up, we knew these guys, we had relationships with them, and we respected them as people, not just policemen. It was a much better way of doing things. When one of those guys stopped you, they had credibility. You wouldn't dream of giving them any lip. When they told you to get home, you'd get home. It's a lot different now. Kids don't like the police.

Mike Modano was spotted by a bird dog. Modano ended up having a twenty-year NHL career with Minnesota and Dallas, and was one of the first American players to come up through the junior hockey system in Canada. A bird dog in Prince Albert knew someone close to Mike – his coach, or maybe a relative. Mike's camp let it be known that he wanted to come to Canada and play junior hockey, and because Prince Albert had a connection, they got him.

That couldn't happen today because the various junior hockey leagues have protected territories that only they can recruit from. For the Western Hockey League it's the western U.S., for the Ontario Hockey League it's the central U.S., and the Quebec Hockey League owns the eastern states. But that division was only established in the last ten years.

When I started playing, and even in Modano's time, having kids in junior hockey from the U.S. was very rare. The American kids were playing college hockey in the U.S., and the Canadian kids were playing junior hockey in Canada. I was actually offered a college scholarship by Minnesota-Duluth when I was seventeen. I never even considered it; I'm not even sure I told my parents about it. It was halfway through the season, and these college recruiters called four of us into the room. The other three guys were older than me. The recruiters said they liked the four of us and laid out the offer. I left the room and told Dwight no thanks. I was so naive. What if I had gotten hurt the next day and couldn't play anymore? I had just turned down a full ride to a very good college in the U.S.

Luckily, I never had to regret that decision. I had a really good junior career. I never had a bad injury, just the usual cuts and bruises you get from playing without a mask. I played for good teams and great guys. There weren't even too many negative days in my junior career. I was getting paid to play hockey. What could be better for a guy who loved the sport and wanted to play in the NHL?

College hockey produces a lot of NHL players now, but in the early '70s, when I was playing, that wasn't the case. At that time, there weren't a lot of American college players making the NHL. The majority of NHL players came from Canadian junior hockey. This was because junior hockey involved playing a seventy-to-eighty-game season – just like the NHL teams – with all the same rules, fighting included. American college hockey played only a thirty-game season, and fighting was illegal. Those guys weren't prepared for the NHL. I thought the U.S. version was a real wimpy game. The feeling in Canada was that American college guys didn't have the guts to play junior hockey.

In the mid-1970s, I met my first U.S. skaters, two Alaskan guys. They might have been the only two American kids in our league. They were tough kids, good players. These two guys came all the way from Anchorage. They drove the whole way without any guarantee they'd make the team. All of a sudden, I realized, "Hey, these guys are no different than me!" I remember it shocked me that there were good hockey players from someplace other than Canada. Of course, geographically, Alaska may as well be Canada.

There really is a definite stereotype that connects how you play with where you are from. I started noticing that when I turned pro and started playing with kids from different areas of the U.S. For instance Minnesota teams play differently than Michigan or Boston teams. The Minnesota kids always played a very highly skilled game, a very fast game, wide open, without a lot of physical play. The Michigan kids were a little tougher, a little more likely to be all-around hockey players. And the Boston kids were very tough: mean and aggressive.

Boston is a very competitive hockey environment. There are a lot of great hockey schools there. It starts in the high schools and continues into the college ranks. Everybody playing hockey knows each other growing up. You can certainly see where the animosity and the aggressiveness come from with Boston teams.

The summer camp I had attended in Weyburn was held to find kids good enough to move on to the final selection process. Ten of us out of fifty made it. The main camp was held a couple of weeks after school started. I'd go to school in the morning and attend the camp in the afternoon. I didn't have a car, but Weyburn was small enough that I could walk everywhere.

We'd have two sessions every afternoon, each running an hour and a half. We mostly scrimmaged, because that's the quickest way to find out if a guy's any good. We were divided into teams and just played against each other. They figured they could work on our fundamentals later.

On any junior team, you'll have a couple of young guys to help with the rebuilding process. I was one of them. At the other end, there will be a couple of twenty-year-olds. In fact, you're only allowed so many twenty-year-olds on the roster because too many could create an unfair advantage. The majority of the players are eighteen or nineteen. When players are in that age range, the first thing you've got to find out is if they can play hockey. That's where all the scrimmaging came in. Dwight picked the twenty guys he liked the most based on how we did in the scrimmages, me included.

Those scrimmages were just like league games, because we were all playing for our futures. We all wanted the same things: to play junior hockey, to play for Weyburn, and to eventually make the NHL. The competition at camp was intense. This was Dwight's first year as coach. The team hadn't been very good the year before, and he was going to make lots of changes. There were about sixty guys at this main camp. Forty were going to be cut to make a roster of twenty. And all of them were good hockey players.

Today, the camps aren't as big because of cost. Nowadays there are thirty-five to forty guys at a camp, but they're still very competitive, and for the same reason. These guys want to play junior hockey, they want to move on, they want to get college scholarships. This is part of an apprenticeship, just like in any other craft.

You want to stand out at camp, make your presence known to everyone. If you're grabbing another player's attention, you're certainly grabbing the management's attention. When kids today ask me what they should do when they go to camp, here's what I tell them: get noticed. Do something to get noticed.

I got noticed because of the way I hit. I was a very physical player, a good hitter, a good bodychecker. I had a knack for timing my hits. I could see when a guy was carrying the puck with his head down. I have always been good at that. I was able to throw some big bodychecks and play in a very physical style. That worked out well for me.

But it was tough. There was fighting, and it was a tough year. Hockey was different then. It was more violent. If my mother had come to camp, she would have taken me home. I had gotten big at age fifteen – six foot one, maybe six-two – but I wasn't a man, I was still a boy. I was playing against men who were between eighteen and twenty years old, and I'd never had to do that before. I'd been hitting and fighting since I started playing – but these guys were all much better players. They were not only older and stronger than me, but more experienced. It took a while to get used to that.

I remember getting crosschecked in the yap early on. Other players would test you to see if you'd stand up for yourself. A lot of guys stayed away from me because I was big and physical. Even the older guys. But still, I'd take some hits. And you had to answer the bell when the time came. If someone crosschecked you, tripped you, or messed with you in some other way, you couldn't just turn your back. You had to go after them. It didn't matter whether you won or lost a fight. You had to stand up for yourself. The only way you could lose a fight was by not fighting.

After a game, there were no hard feelings, no carryover, no anger. Both guys knew it was just part of the game. You'd fight a guy on the ice, and that night you'd be eating together, or watching TV with him at somebody's place. Everything was forgotten. That's what people don't realize about fighting in hockey. You're not mad when you fight. It's a job, something that you have to do. You are either sending a message, or you're trying to intimidate the other team – or maybe a particular player – or you're standing up for one of your players or yourself. Very rarely do you fight because you're mad. In fact, the worst fighters are the guys who do get mad during a fight. Good fighters are the guys who just see it as a job.

It's not legal to fight in any other sport, so it's difficult for people who don't play hockey to realize that fighting is a tool. Used properly, it's a good tool. It may seem crazy to say, but fighting actually takes a lot of violence out of our sport. Chances are that if you really drilled somebody back then, you were going to have to stand up right at that moment and fight somebody, defend yourself. These days, there is not so much fighting, so everybody on the ice hits because they know nothing will happen to them. There are guys who have no courage at all who are delivering marginally cheap hits because they know they can get away with them. Fighting reduced cheap shots, high-sticking, and hits to the head. Fighting has kept a lid on our sport. I personally think it's a healthy part of our game.

Other sports could profit from fighting. In baseball, when a pitcher throws at a batter, if that batter were allowed to charge the mound and tangle with the guy who just threw a hard-as-a-rock ball at his head at ninety miles an hour, you would have a lot fewer pitchers throwing at batters. And the fighting in hockey is exciting as hell. I don't think we should get rid of stuff that is exciting.

My dad had no problem with me fighting. We never once discussed me not doing it. I'll remember that forever. My dad never once thought that I wouldn't have to fight. He was great with it, my grandfather was great with it, but I found out later that my mother cried for three days after I left for Weyburn.

The first junior game she ever came to, I was in two fights. I got my nose bloodied real bad. I was a bleeder. If someone popped me in the nose, my nose bled like a pig. As a kid, I once had the doctor cauterize the inside of my nose to try and stop it from bleeding so badly. But that night, I was happier than hell out there. I was a member of the team, I was fighting, everyone was patting me on the back, I was like a warrior. But my mother was very upset after the game.

I didn't know how upset she was at the time. I found out much later from my dad. She was one of those women who didn't show her emotions to her children. But after the game, Dad said she was furious. She was angry at me, she was angry at Weyburn. She knew it would be tough, but I don't think she envisioned her son fighting twice in one game, her fifteen-year-old kid fighting these *men*. She'd seen me fight before, but it was always against guys my own age. That aspect of it caught her by surprise. She was shocked, really. She wasn't ready for how tough, mean, and nasty junior hockey was.

Her outburst was pretty much over by the time I'd showered, dressed, and joined my family. But right after the game, she had told my dad and grandfather that I was going to be pulled from Weyburn and taken home. She was adamant about it. They had some job settling her down and making her realize I was doing what I wanted, and that we'd all talked about it.

There weren't many negative things about Weyburn. My mother liked Dwight a lot, thank heavens. If there had been a coach she didn't like, or if I hadn't been doing well at school, she would have been tough to convince. And she knew I had to fight; she knew that's how I had to play. By the time I showed up, she was ready to give me the old speech – I don't like it, but you make sure your marks stay up, and listen to Dwight, work hard every day. So we got through it.

Going into junior hockey, the first thing a young player has to understand is the business aspect of it. That's hard for a fifteen-year-old. If I'd gone to camp and been terrible, they would've cut me, sent me home. Even after I made the team, I could have been traded or cut at any time. It's tough for the kids, but just as hard on the coaches. When I coached junior, I had to bring sixteen-year-olds into my office and tell them they'd been traded or cut. It was so hard on them, they'd often start crying.

In Weyburn, there were two other kids my age playing on the junior team. One of them settled in Weyburn and is still one of my good friends. The other kid was brought in early, same as me, and put in school. He was brutal in camp and brutal in the games. Brutal means bad. He just wasn't working very hard. They sent him back home after about two months. I'm not sure why he didn't perform. He might not have been ready to move away from home. Leaving home was very traumatic for some kids. Some very good players didn't make it for that reason. But whatever Dwight had seen in this boy in the summer, he didn't bring with him in the fall.

They gave all of us a little bit of spending money depending on how long we'd been there. As a fifteen-year-old rookie, I got about seventy-five dollars a month. Even the guys that were nineteen or twenty years old were only getting two hundred and fifty dollars a month. If you weren't in school, they tried to get you jobs. Nobody was getting rich.

Every time my grandfather saw me, he put twenty in my pocket. My dad did the same thing. You could eat and buy toothpaste on what the team gave you, but you had no spending money if your parents weren't helping you out.

My first year at Weyburn went well. I played pretty regularly, and I got better as the year went on. At the beginning, though, it wasn't easy. I was often on the bench, sitting it out. I'll never forget one game in particular.

Weyburn went up to play Yorkton, the closest team to Kelvington. Two buses full of people from home came to the game because there were three Kelvington kids playing that night: two kids on the Yorkton team, and me. There must have been 120 people from Kelvington at this game – my mom and dad included. I did nothing but warm the bench. I sat out the entire game. It was hard to believe, but Dwight didn't play me one single shift. It was one of the worst days of my life. I've known Dwight forty years, and we're still friends, but I have never asked him why he didn't play me in that game – I guess I never will ask him. As a coach, I've had to do the same sort of thing to players I really liked. Situations happen, or you're teaching the kid something, you're sending a message.

Maybe a guy isn't practising well. When I coached, I insisted on having good practices. Good play doesn't just happen. If you practise hard and fast, then you'll start playing that way. If I had to speak with a player about improving the way he was practising, and he still wasn't making an effort, I'd dress him and not play him much. Or I'd keep him on the bench two periods and see how he responded in the third. The only power a coach really has is ice time. It's a tool, because it's a commodity players want.

Whatever the reason, that night in Yorkton, Dwight thought it was better for me not to play in that game. That was one long game, and Yorkton won, so it was a bad night for Barry Melrose all around.

I've never figured it out. Dwight was never mad at me. Maybe he felt I would've been too nervous. I don't know. Maybe it was a teaching moment. Maybe it made me hungrier. Maybe it was a kick in the butt that made me work harder. I probably *should* ask him. But he thought it was right and he usually did the right thing.

I never wanted such a thing to happen again. It was embarrassing. All those people I had grown up with were sitting in the stands. I'm sure everybody thought I was going to be cut or traded after that night. They didn't understand the workings of a junior hockey team. They didn't know that coaches sent messages or did things like that for a reason. I'm sure it was a long drive home for my mom and dad on that bus, sitting there with all their friends and neighbours.

As the year went on, I got stronger and stronger. By the end of that season, I was sixteen years old and playing regularly. That was unusual in that league because there weren't that many kids my age taking regular shifts in junior hockey.

Weyburn made the playoffs. We got beaten by Estevan in the first round, but given that it was Dwight's first year with a junior team, we had accomplished a lot. We had one of the better teams in the Saskatchewan Junior Hockey League, and we had a good series against a very tough team. I think we lost in six games.

Dwight changed the culture at Weyburn. Before he took over, Weyburn had been a very undisciplined group. The boys were in trouble a lot. Dwight changed all that. He made sure that he only kept kids on the team who were serious enough about hockey to behave themselves. Weyburn became a good hockey town with a team that was well coached, very well disciplined; a team that had a game plan and a good model. Dwight coaches his teams the same way to this day.

I remember the playoffs. I had good games against Estevan, our hated rival. I was in two fights, and I did great against older players. I got two black eyes, but I held my own. Matter of fact, one of the guys I fought ended up with a black eye, too. The next game, we were skating in the warmup and he and I made eye contact. He was nineteen years old, a pretty big guy, and he had this very handsome black eye. We didn't exactly exchange smiles, but we were both looking at each others' shiners and probably feeling the same thing: that we were giving as good as we got.

There's respect involved. When all those guys at Estevan saw me fight twice and do well in both fights, they started playing differently against me. I'd sent a message, and so they were very careful around me. They didn't take liberties or try any cheap shots. That was a good lesson about how to present yourself on the ice.

One of the best things about coaching is seeing a kid change and improve his game. You see the kid get more physical, watch the confidence rising in him, and you smile at how his style of play changes as a result. You see him evolving into a really good player. That's what I loved about coaching junior hockey. I know Dwight felt the same way when he was watching me evolve into a better player.

Being traded was a spectre that was always in the back of our minds in junior. They could have come in anytime and told me they were trading me to Prince Albert or somewhere else. And I would have had to go. It's very hard, because at age sixteen you commit to the team, and they commit to you.

Later on, as a coach, I'd walk into the houses of these young kids and tell the parents I was going to do this and that, and then down the road the boy would be traded. I had to do it a couple times. It's a very unpleasant part of the job. It's easy to trade kids you don't like, but sometimes you have to trade kids you do like. That's no fun at all.

That first year I was in Weyburn, I saw teammates get traded. I knew it could happen to me, but I didn't really believe it would. In the back of my mind, I knew I *could* be traded some day. In fact, I have been traded a few times in my career. That nagging possibility is always there, but you don't think about it. You can't think about it. Once you get into the profession, you just have to roll with the punches. If it happens, it happens. You just have to keep playing your best. I always figured if I played my best, it would take care of all the problems.

When a kid did get traded, it created major turmoil in that teenager's life. I've seen guys with steady girlfriends refuse to be traded and quit the game. It never occurred to me that anyone would do that. For me, hockey always came first. Signing with Weyburn was probably the biggest decision I made in my life, because from that point forward I made a living from hockey. I knew I wanted to play hockey. That's all I ever wanted to do. Ever since Dad and I came to the decision that I would move to Weyburn and start school, I played hockey nine months a year until I went into coaching. That decision was a defining moment in my life, no question.

3

Dark Ages

I played for Weyburn two years. My second year there, when I was seventeen, I made the all-star team. I had one particularly good home game toward the end of that year. I scored a goal, had some big hits, and was in two fights.

That night, my dad called me and said he'd heard a scout from the New Westminster Bruins interviewed on the radio. New Westminster was in the Western Hockey League, which is a significant step up from the Saskatchewan Junior Hockey League that Weyburn played in at the time. My dad said they had interviewed the scout on the air and asked him what he was doing in Weyburn, and he said he had come to watch Barry Melrose play. He said he hoped I would be playing for New Westminster next year, that they were really looking forward to having me in their lineup.

I found out later that New Westminster had actually come to Dwight halfway through my second year and wanted to take me right then. But Dwight had promised my mom he would hold on to me for two years so I could finish high school, but that after that I would probably be gone. He was right.

The WHL is part of the Canadian Hockey League, a national organization that also includes teams in Pennsylvania, Washington state, Oregon, and Michigan on the U.S. side. The CHL is an umbrella organization that represents a total of sixty teams in three conferences: the Western Hockey League, the Ontario Hockey League, and the Quebec Major Junior Hockey League.

The way it worked back then was teams that saw you first put you on their "protected list." Each team had a list of seventy players – a seventy-spot list, it was called. It was later reduced to fifty spots. Scouts, often prompted by bird dogs, would see a kid they liked and would call the team's GM, telling him to put the boy on his spot list. Thirteen-year-olds would take up three spots. Fourteen-year-olds would take up two spots. Older kids took up one spot. A team also had to keep a thirteen-year-old on its list for six months. That prevented teams from throwing a kid on the list and dumping him a day later. Players and spots were all tradable items. It was a tricky game. The master list was kept in the league office. Every team had access to the other teams' lists, but otherwise they were unpublished. If two teams saw a player they liked, the one who called the league office first got him, simple as that. That system was used for a long time.

It all ended with what they called the bantam draft in 1990. Every bantam player in western Canada and the U.S. was put into a draft, and the team that finished last got the first pick, just like in the NHL. There is still a fifty-spot list populated by players that don't make the draft, but the bantam draft established a more level playing field. Up to then, the best-organized teams ruled. They had the best scouting systems and were first to discover the good young players.

New Westminster, which is part of Greater Vancouver, was the first team that saw me. They owned my rights. But I never made it to New Westminster because, during the summer, they traded my rights to Kamloops, British Columbia, a city of ninety-five thousand people about two hundred miles northeast of Vancouver. All this went on without my participation.

It was difficult for me because I really enjoyed Weyburn. I had made a lot of really close friends there. It was a big move. Kamloops was a fifteen-hour drive west, and I'd never been to British Columbia. When I was in Weyburn, my parents could easily come to a game. But in Kamloops, the only places they could come see me play were Saskatoon and maybe Regina, and we only played in those towns once a season. It would be a lot harder on my family.

To be honest, the Western Hockey League was a little scary. If the Saskatchewan Junior Hockey League was tough, the WHL had a reputation of being twenty times tougher. As young kids, we grew up in awe of the Western league. I had some sleepless nights about whether I was good enough to make the step up.

The good thing was that Kamloops was an expansion team. Officially the team was two years old. They had played in Vancouver as the Nats before moving to Kamloops. But it was their first year in the WHL, so we were all new to the upgrade. That kept me from being one of the new guys who might get singled out for heavy testing. They had several boys who'd played on a Kamloops Tier II team. Back then Weyburn and the other teams in the Saskatchewan league were in Tier II, a division for guys who weren't as good, or who were trying to get hockey scholarships in the U.S. If the latter group were to play in the WHL, which was Tier I, they would have been ineligible.

U.S. colleges consider the WHL as having professional status, that's how good it is. The Tier I kids were also being paid a stipend, which made them ineligible for scholarships. Today the two tiers are known as major junior and provincial junior A.

Training camp was a whole new experience for me. The guys were bigger, stronger, and obviously better. I made it because I was determined. My goal was always to play in the NHL. I knew Kamloops was a stepping stone to that end, but it was hard leaving Weyburn, no doubt about it.

Players from the Western Hockey League often stepped right into the NHL. Some of the best players in the world have done that – guys like Bryan Trottier (New York Islanders) and Barry Beck (New York Rangers). I had done well in the Saskatchewan Junior league, making the all-star team, but you always wonder if you can survive at the next level. I got to training camp and saw right away that everyone was bigger and faster than the guys I'd been playing with. The quality of the games was also better. But I soon realized I could play with these guys, and that gave me confidence. I've also always made friends easily. Some of the guys I played with there are some of the best friends I ever had.

One thing I remember about that training camp is that I was in terrible condition. That summer, I didn't work out as much as I should have. At Weyburn, there was no off-ice training, no running, nothing like that. When I got to Kamloops, they had this trainer – I'll never forget the guy's name: Don Bush. Don was a physical fitness nut. He ran us nearly to death.

We had to do physical fitness tests, pull-ups, push-ups. All of that was new to me. He had us running miles, flying around the track every day. It about killed me. That was one of the most physically challenging weeks of my life, that first week in Kamloops, because of the off-ice training.

And it was hot – hotter in Kamloops in September than it was in Saskatchewan in July. Running in the heat was murder. I'd never had to run before. This was 1974, when hockey was changing, with physical fitness becoming a much bigger factor. Off-ice training was the new thing. I'll remember for the rest of my life how hard that was. It wasn't my best moment, let's put it that way.

But it was also a great teaching tool because I never went to camp in poor shape again. After that, I ran every summer and always showed up in great shape. It was a tough love–type deal, a shock to my system, a wake-up call. I never wanted to feel that out of shape again, or be that embarrassed, or be unprepared physically ever again for anything.

There was a wonderful woman in Kamloops named Doris Rubel who ran all the billets there for forty years. She kept everybody in line, made sure everyone got along. She was a great matchmaker, with a knack for putting the right kids with the right families. Mrs. Rubel found me a great place to stay. Three of us billeted with the same family, and it was a terrific situation. I'm still friends with that family to this day. It's a great system that's been working a long time, thanks to people like Doris Rubel. We lost her in the summer of 2011. That was a very sad loss for junior hockey.

As it happened, my first game with Kamloops was against New Westminster. It was an exhibition game played in Revelstoke,

British Columbia, three hours east of Kamloops. It turned out to be a wild game full of fights. The Revelstoke rink was old, dark, and dingy. I remember being out warming up and looking across the rink and seeing this gigantic team step out onto the ice. They were all six foot three, four, or five, and they wore black, like the Boston Bruins. In that dark, old building it looked like a horror movie. I'm a big guy, and there were ten New West players bigger than me. That was my first impression of the Western Hockey League. It looked like it was going to be a long night.

We lined up to start the game, and there's Harold Phillipoff, whom I'd been playing hockey and baseball against since we were twelve years old. Harold was from Canora, a town near Kelvington in Saskatchewan. Harold was a huge guy New West had drafted as a fighter. It happened that we lined up together. Just before the first drop of the puck, Harold turned to me and said, "Pretty fuckin' big team, eh?"

New Westminster's team was terribly tough. They'd modelled themselves after the Philadelphia Flyers of the NHL. They were bigger than a lot of NHL teams, and in those days – the mid-'70s – we were playing under basic prison rules. It was a tough time to play hockey, a scary time to play hockey.

Coming up against New Westminster was my baptism by fire into the Western Hockey League. I realized that was how it was going to be for the next two years.

In the NHL, the Flyers were king. They had put a big emphasis on intimidation and toughness, and it won them two Stanley Cups. The success of that style of play permeated all of hockey for about ten years. A lot of kids chose not to play in those days because of how tough it was.

Those years were the Dark Ages. There were many fights every game, and line brawls every night. A line brawl is when all five guys on the ice are fighting at one time – sometimes even the goalies got involved. Bench-clearing brawls were also common. There'd be more guys in the penalty box than on the bench. Hockey in those years was crazy. It started changing back to more of a skill game in the '80s, but the '70s were a dark decade for the NHL, and for all of hockey.

The Flyers were an expansion team that came into the NHL in 1967. Because of the restrictions put on new teams in the expansion, they weren't able to quickly attain the talent level of teams like Montreal or Boston, so they decided they were going to compete by changing the way the game was played. They had a few really good players – Bobby Clarke, Reggie Leach, Rick MacLeish, Billy Barber – but instead of trying to add more talent to compete successfully with Montreal, who had set the standard for artfully played hockey, they went in a different direction.

The Flyers went out and got some of the toughest guys in hockey: Dave Schultz, Bob "Hound Dog" Kelly, Don Saleski, Ed Van Impe, Moose Dupont. Those were real tough guys. With them on the roster, the Flyers started using fighting and violence as tools. Instead of trying to beat you with their skill level, they intimidated teams with their toughness. And it worked.

Philadelphia had brought in Fred Shero as coach. Fred was a genius. He took the Flyers to the Stanley Cup finals three times, and won it twice (1974, 1975). He was the first coach to hire a full-time assistant for himself, first to use in-season strength training, and he introduced the morning skate, which all teams use now.

Fred used the morning skate as a warmup. Everyone would come out in sweatpants. The only person wearing equipment was the goalie. You would hit him with the puck a few times, break a little sweat, and that would be it. Half an hour and you were done. Fred used morning skates mainly to get his team out of bed. He didn't want them sleeping until noon. The morning skate has changed over the years. It can be really strenuous, with full pads, full contact, and can last almost an hour. These days, it's often a teaching session, with teams going over videos of past games, making adjustments. It's also a chance for trainers to work with guys who are injured. The morning skate has evolved into an important part of conditioning and training.

At the direction of Flyers management, Fred also took the game to a new level of violence. All of a sudden, instead of trying to win games with lots of talented players, Philly would outfight you. They intimidated teams, they really did. Then, in 1974, they won the Cup.

At that point, everybody figured that to win the Cup, they had to beat Philadelphia at their own game. It was like an arms escalation, very similar to Russia and the United States continually upping the ante on missiles during the Cold War. For a ten-year period, every team tried to be the toughest team in the NHL. That's when the movie *Slap Shot* came out and glorified hockey as a blood sport. Every team had several goons. There'd be five guys on a team's roster who did nothing but fight.

The Flyers ushered in the Dark Ages because they were winning with that style of hockey. You know the old saying, "If you can't beat 'em, join 'em," so everybody had to get tougher in order to play the Flyers. One team starts winning with a different style of play, and all of a sudden every team starts copying them. There was a big cycle of goon hockey there for about ten years all throughout the NHL, the American Hockey League, and yes, also in junior hockey.

In the NHL in those days, the top picks were always fighters. The first-round draft picks weren't skill guys, they were the tough guys. One was Harold Phillipoff, the guy I knew back in Saskatchewan. Harold and I got drafted the same year, 1976. He was a huge guy, not a very good hockey player, who was drafted in the first round by Atlanta because of his fighting ability. Other tough guys drafted in the first round were: Steve Durbano (1974 – St. Louis); Rick Chartraw (1974 – Montreal); Cam Connor (1974 – Montreal); and Jimmy Mann (1979 – Winnipeg). Combined, those guys managed just sixty goals in 1022 NHL games, but served over twenty-five hundred minutes in penalties during that time.

Montreal was toughing up their lineup, like every other team in that era. But it was the Canadiens' return to a skill game in the late '70s that set things right again. Their success ended the goon cycle, forcing the other teams to go back to an emphasis on skill. Then the Edmonton Oilers started winning with players like Wayne Gretzky, and everybody wanted skilled guys and fast skaters on their teams again.

Management didn't do anything about the Dark Ages because Philadelphia was winning and because there is a huge segment of fans who love the violence. The buildings were full. Business was good. So the NHL let it ride. They had to put a face of disapproval on it, but nothing was really done, not until talent started winning again – not until Montreal and Edmonton started winning and hockey management realized they had to change.

There were some protests during that time. Bobby Hull was playing in the World Hockey Association by then. He staged a protest against the violence by sitting out three games. But did the NHL or WHA adopt hard rules to combat the violence? No, they didn't. Neither did junior hockey or any other leagues. The violence was selling tickets. The business model was working. People can say they hate fighting and they hate violence, but did you ever see someone at a game get up and leave during a fight? I never have.

Hockey is a very violent game. When you hit someone, you are trying to hurt them, make them feel it. It's the same in football. When a guy carries the ball across the middle and one of the linebackers hits him, they are trying to hurt him, send a message. You want to make him think twice the next time he gets the ball, maybe make him hesitate even a little. So yes, when you hit someone on the open ice, you're trying to sting them.

I don't think it's the mentality of hockey players to want to really damage people. We're all athletes and professionals. We're trying to win. We'll do just about *anything* to win, but do we want to put guys in the hospital? No. Do we want them to pay a price? Yes.

It was discovered in the spring of 2012 that the New Orleans Saints had been using a bounty system for hits that knocked opposing players out of games. That was surprising to a lot of us, because that approach is not within the spirit of professional sports. I've been involved in organized hockey at every level since I was fifteen, and I never once heard of anyone being paid to hurt someone. That's not how or why hockey players play the game.

Both football and hockey are violent sports. But the athletes from both leagues are in professional associations, and all of them are trying to make a living for themselves and their families. It makes no sense at all to try and end someone's career, or, for that matter, to hurt someone who just might be your teammate in a couple of months.

You hit somebody to make him change the way he plays, to intimidate him. If you sting him, maybe the next time the guy comes in on you, he'll give up the puck. That is why you hit. If you hit a really talented guy a couple of times, then maybe he doesn't want the puck so much anymore, and it changes his game, makes him less of a threat.

There's much more headhunting today because there are no repercussions. Believe it or not, when I was playing, if I high-sticked someone or hit him in the head, or if someone high-sticked me, there would be a fight – right then. Not many players did those things, because they didn't want to fight. In 2012, there's not so much fighting in the NHL anymore.

Every night on ESPN's *SportsCenter,* you're seeing hits to the head, and you're seeing suspensions coming from the league office as a result. Everybody carries his stick high and everybody hits to the head because they know nothing will happen directly to them. Sure, they might get fined, or they might get suspended, but they're never going to have to stand up and be physically accountable for their actions. That's one of the changes in the game that's been caused by having fighting virtually eliminated.

Back to the Dark Ages: there really is a line between intimidation and assault. Hockey is a game played with long, whippy sticks and a puck as hard as a rock, on skates with blades sharp enough to shave ice or plane wood. That line is crossed at times. There is good hard, physical hockey – courageous hockey – and there is a moment when all-out violence enters in. There is a line, and sometimes it's blurred.

If a player got suspended during the Dark Ages, then the guy he hit had to almost have died. To get suspended in those days, you had to do something really bad, like knock somebody senseless. And there *was* plenty of stuff like that going on because suspensions were commonplace in those days, not a rarity. But the suspensions did little to stop the brutal hits and brawls. It was a vicious time. People say today's game is violent. The Dark Ages are beyond comparison for violence.

Most nights, if you were a fan back then, you were surprised if there wasn't a bench-clearing brawl. Guys would say, "Hey, I can't believe there wasn't a brawl tonight. What's happening? Is this game getting soft?"

In that era, intimidation qualified as a game plan. We'd actually go over the opposing lineup before the game and talk about who could be intimidated. Then we'd use rough stuff to scare the other team, to scare certain players.

In Kamloops, we traveled exclusively by bus. We virtually lived on the bus. Our shortest trip was to New Westminster – and that was five hours. There were some long trips – fifteen, twenty hours – and believe me those buses we traveled in were just boxes on wheels. Nowadays, the buses have DVD players and sleepers. Back then, you were lucky if there was a bathroom in the bus. We used to drive all across Canada. Guys would be sleeping on the luggage racks over the seats, on the floor, or sleeping crushed up in the seats. It was amazing how you could fit yourself into different areas to get some sleep. I was very lucky in that I could sleep on the bus. To this day, I can get in any vehicle and quickly fall asleep. But those were long, long trips. I look back now and I just shake my head thinking about it.

We would travel five or ten hours, play, then drive back. You'd get up in the morning and travel to New Westminster in time for a game at seven o'clock, play, then get back on the bus and arrive home at three or four in the morning. I was done school by then, but some of the guys were still working on their high school credits. Good luck.

I didn't have time to think about college, or even junior college. First of all, the minute you started playing in the WHL, you lost your eligibility for a scholarship. I could have kept playing for Weyburn in the Saskatchewan Junior Hockey League and still gotten a scholarship, but like I said, I didn't want to play U.S. college hockey. In junior, we played the same number of games the NHL did. On a road trip, we would play Edmonton, Calgary, Regina, Saskatoon, Brandon, Winnipeg, Flin Flon – seven games in ten nights, all travelling by bus. And we weren't staying in great hotels, either. We were staying in little mom-and-pop no-tell motels on the sides of the highways. I look back on it fondly, but it was crazy.

The team would provide sandwiches and chips on the bus after a game, so you'd just get on the bus and leave, and eat sandwiches on the road. Very rarely did we stop as a team to eat, it was basically just grab and go. Nutritionists today would be horrified at what we ate. Every once in a while, we'd stop at a restaurant. They'd have to set it up ahead of time because there's no way they could serve twenty-five hungry hockey players if they weren't ready for us. We'd eat like crazy, be finished and back on the bus in half an hour, but those dinners were few and far between.

There was one place where teams stopped to eat, halfway to New Westminster. New West was so tough back then everyone was scared to play them. So players would lock themselves in the bathroom and pretend they got locked in by accident so that they would miss the bus to New Westminster. Other guys would get mysteriously sick on the way there. We called it the New West flu. It was the WHL version of the Philly Flu in the NHL. That's how serious intimidation works. Guys did not want to play the New Westminster Bruins because they feared getting hurt.

I didn't look at our tight schedule or all the travel on the terrible buses as either good or bad. It was just the way it was. I was playing hockey, and that was all I cared about. I enjoyed going to Saskatchewan and Manitoba, because that gave my mom and dad a chance to see me play.

In my four years in junior hockey, first in Weyburn, then in Kamloops, I don't recall missing a game. Again, I was very lucky. While I was playing for Kamloops, we had a bus accident in the mountains. Our bus went off the road on the ice and crashed. I was actually thrown through the front window. I got a bad cut on my leg, but it didn't stop me from playing. In fact, two nights later, I played against the Russian national team. I do realize that, given all the goon squad stuff that was going on in those years, it's truly amazing that I never got hurt badly enough to miss a game. After that bus accident, it was the trainer who took care of my leg. In the Western Hockey League, the trainer was the medical man, the equipment man, the teacher . . . he was everything. Medicine Hat's trainer was famous. His name was Bob Ridley. He would drive the team to the games, help unload the bus, then run up to the booth and do the radio broadcast by himself, play-by-play and colour. After the game, he'd help load the bus and drive home. He did that for forty years. His love of hockey made for a strong commitment.

Our trainer in Weyburn had been Doc Bathe. He worked for all the town's sports teams. When I got to Weyburn, Doc was eighty years old. He had served in World War I, and whenever he'd get mad at us, he'd give us a going over: "You bastards think you're tough? In WWI, I got five horses shot out from under me in one battle. . . . You're a bunch of pussies, a bunch of wimps." Doc was a great guy, a unique individual. There were many like him in hockey. It seemed every place I went, every city and every town would have some hard-working guy like Doc who was dedicated to the local team.

Doc was another do-everything guy. At eighty, he'd be carrying our jerseys home to wash at his house. I mean carrying, by himself, and those things were heavy. Here's an eighty-year-old man carrying the jerseys home on his back in the middle of winter to wash in his own washing machine so they'd be clean for the next game.

He was the medical man, too. You never wanted to get a charley horse around Doc. He'd always have a silver dollar in his pocket that he would use to bring the knot out of your muscle. It was one of those things where the cure was worse than the affliction. You'd almost rather play with a charley horse than get Doc to bring out that silver dollar. He almost relished it. You could see him thinking, "How much can I make this kid hurt?"

He stood the silver dollar on end and ground it into your leg, into the muscle. When he brought that silver dollar out of his pocket, you knew what hell was going to feel like if you went there. All of us would make a circle around the patient and watch Doc go in there and bring that charley horse out of this guy's leg or thigh, and it was worth the price of admission.

Junior hockey depends on volunteers for all sorts of things, but the billeting is most important. Every junior hockey town and city has people who open up their homes to young players year after year and make them part of their families. No junior team could exist if that didn't happen, because teams don't have the money to put players up in hotels and apartments. The billets get paid, but not much. All of them lose money. When I was playing, the billets got a hundred and fifty dollars a month for each player, and that didn't even begin to feed a hungry junior hockey player. And these people did our laundry, made the beds, and were generally there for us. They weren't doing it for the money, I'll guarantee that.

4

Horns of a Dilemma

I loved Kamloops. It's a gorgeous city on the Thompson River in the lee of the Coast Mountains, and a great sports town, a great hockey town. I had wonderful friends there and a nice billet. The Kamloops Cheifs were among the better teams in the WHL. It was a fun two years of my life. I was playing well, getting some notoriety, moving toward my goal of playing in the NHL. I made the all-star team my second year in Kamloops, and really felt good about the direction I was going. Junior hockey was a great four years of my life. A lot of the guys I played with in junior are still close friends of mine today.

I got drafted after my second season in Kamloops. The NHL draft wasn't on television back then; they did everything over the phone. It was held in June, two weeks after the Stanley Cup finals were over. I was back home in Kelvington, and I was really nervous that day, so I got on the tractor and went out in the field. I was working all morning, which was much better than hanging around waiting for a call from my agent.

Every time I think about how I got that agent, I get angry. In Kamloops, our coach and general manager brought half a dozen players who they thought might be drafted into a room. This man was standing there. We were all told, "This is your agent." That's exactly what happened. He was going to represent all of us. And all of us said, "Okay." We just accepted it, that's how naive we were. That was our hockey mentality. I was always taught that we could trust adults – that they would look out for you. And growing up, they had.

We had been taught to trust our coaches. I'd just come from Weyburn, where my coach, Dwight MacMillan, had taken great care of me. On graduation night, I wrecked my car and got banged up pretty bad. Dwight went out and took care of my car, and was the first guy who came to see me in the hospital. He even phoned my parents. Kamloops was different.

We trusted the coach and GM, figuring they were going to do the best thing for us. We found out later that money had changed hands. I look back at that situation with bitterness. The coach and GM should have been looking out for us. Instead, they were accepting money from agents to have players sign with them.

When I became a coach, I made sure I was always looking out for the players, doing the best for them. If they came to me and asked me about a particular agent, I'd offer my opinion if I knew the guy, and urge them to do careful research, look into it first hand.

A few years later, my roommate had an agent who was always phoning him. My agent rarely called me. He just took his percentage. One night, we were out with my friend's agent. I spoke with him, told him the situation, and he agreed to represent me. The first thing he did was look at my contract. He found an annual kickback of six thousand dollars that was going to my junior club. He said that had been going on since the first year of my contract. He fixed that, and from then on, the money came to me.

I figured to be drafted, but I didn't have a clue who would take me. Not a clue. So, rather than hang by the phone, I was out in the middle of nowhere on the tractor when I saw my grandfather's car come flying up the road. Saskatchewan's so flat, you can see the dust from a car approaching ten miles away. He came tearing across the field, stopped, got out, and was waving at me like crazy. He was yelling, "Come on, come on! Get in the car, get in the car!" He said my agent was going to be calling in ten minutes to tell me who had drafted me. That's all he knew. It wasn't on the radio, and there was no other notice. He just knew my agent had called and said, "Where's Barry?" He said to go and get me, and he'd call back in twenty minutes.

I got in the house and everybody was already there – my grandma and grandfather, Mom and Dad, brothers and sisters. The phone rang. Everybody got quiet. My agent told me I had been taken in the second round by the Montreal Canadiens. Montreal! What a moment for a kid from Saskatchewan who grew up idolizing one of the greatest teams of all time. But after the initial giddy rush, I realized it was bittersweet. My mom and dad, grandpa, and grandma were all beside themselves. They didn't realize going to Montreal wasn't necessarily all it was cracked up to be.

The Canadiens were the best team in the NHL by far. They would turn out to be the dominant team of the late '70s. Their brand of firewagon hockey would win them four Stanley Cups from 1976 to 1979. They had four all-star defencemen. Their farm team, the Nova Scotia Voyageurs, had just won the American Hockey League championship, and *they* had four all-star defencemen as well. I'd be going into an organization with all those great defencemen ahead of me. That was not good. My mom and dad and grandparents were overcome by Montreal taking me in the second round, but I had been in hockey long enough to see the negative sides of being drafted to a team that loaded with talent.

Regardless, being drafted was great, a real feather in my cap. My dream had been realized. Montreal called, and I spoke with Mr. Pollock – Sam Pollock, the greatest GM in hockey. He had assembled two dynasty teams and had won seven Stanley Cups, with two more to come. His coach was the legendary Scotty Bowman, who has more regular-season and playoff wins than any other coach. They called and said how pleased they were that they had drafted me and all that. It was an honour to speak with them. Those men were like myths to me.

They sent me a contract. Usually, you get a two-way contract that specifies one salary while you play in the NHL, and a much lower one if you get sent down to the American Hockey League. But what they sent me was a *three-way* contract: one salary for the NHL, a much lower one for the AHL, and an even lower salary in case I ended up in the International Hockey

League, still another step down. I have kept that three-way contract in my scrapbook to this day.

I knew that if you signed with an NHL team, they owned you and could send you wherever they wanted. You'd have nothing to say about it. Looking at that three-way contract was when I really started thinking the NHL might not be the best place for me. Luckily, I had another option. The World Hockey Association had drafted me as well.

The WHA was a rebel league that had started in 1972. It was designed to compete with the NHL. The WHA had set up teams in major cities where the NHL didn't have a presence and attracted good players by paying them more – most famously Bobby Hull, who jumped from the NHL to the WHA for a record $2.75 million (for ten years). Unlike the NHL, the WHA didn't have a reserve clause that bound players to teams, so players were free to move around. They had also started signing European players. Sixty-seven NHL players moved to the WHA the first year it was in existence, hoping to capitalize on the higher salaries and increased freedom.

I'd been drafted by the WHA's Cincinnati Stingers in the third round. Cincinnati was a young team that had some great junior players in their system. I spoke with their management, and the team flew me down to look at the city. Generally, they showed more interest in me than the Canadiens. The more I thought about it, the more I realized I probably would have been sent to the IHL by Montreal, whereas if I joined the WHA, there was a good possibility I'd be playing in Cincinnati my first year. Cincinnati started looking more and more attractive. The money was also much better. If I'd been sent to the IHL by Montreal, I would have been making around twelve thousand dollars a year. The first year with Cincinnati, I'd be making thirty-five thousand dollars.

I was on the horns of a dilemma. My life's goal was to play in the NHL, and it didn't get any better than Montreal with all its history, tradition, and glamour – not to mention they were a great team at the time, with terrific management and a famous coach. Being drafted by them was the greatest thing that could ever have happened. It was my dream and then some. But did I have a legitimate shot at playing for the Canadiens?

Cincinnati had flown me in, wined and dined me, taken me to a Reds game. It was my first time in the U.S. I hadn't flown much, or spent any time in a big city like Cincinnati, so it was all an eye-opener for a country boy from the wilds of Canada.

Cincinnati offered me a three-year deal. Their contract was one-way – even if I got sent down to a minor league, I'd be making the same money. So, after all those years of working hard, planning, and dreaming about the NHL, I was thinking of telling them "No thanks" and going to the WHA. My head was spinning.

I was surprised, and also probably grateful, that my mom and dad stayed out of my decision. They just said, "Do what you think is best." It was completely up to me. I made the decision. I think when Cincinnati flew me down, showed a real interest in me, that was what did it. They had been smart. And they had flown two of us from Kamloops down at same time so we could hang out together.

I looked at their lineup, and they had some guys I knew from the Western league who were good young players. Their rink was beautiful, the city was beautiful. So, I signed after I returned from that Cincinnati trip. Thinking back, it wasn't that hard a decision for me. If I had signed with Montreal, that might have looked good on my résumé. But then, I never knew when – or if – I would get to Montreal.

As it happened, I fell in love with Cincinnati, Ohio. I had three great years there. I met my wife there. And I got better every year, so by year end I was an important part of the team. I played a ton, and would have been happy to play there the rest of my career.

The Stingers were young, but a quality team. We could have played in the NHL as an upper-echelon team. Boston and Philadelphia were the elite teams in the NHL back then, but all the WHA teams would have been fighting for a playoff spot if they had been in the NHL. If there had been a tournament between the two leagues, it could have gone either way. When the leagues finally merged, most of us ended up going to the NHL. That was an indication of how good Cincinnati was.

The WHA was no exception to the ultra-violent style of hockey that had been started by the Flyers. The Birmingham Bulls were the equivalent of the Flyers in the WHA. I'll always remember one amazing game we had with them. It was on Valentine's Day, 1978. There was a good crowd, around twelve thousand. Birmingham had a beautiful building that seated around seventeen thousand. It was well lit with a great ice surface, and everything was well maintained.

Both teams lined up at centre ice before the game. A minister walked on the ice and said he would like to give thanks to God for letting us gather here on this beautiful day, for letting us join together and watch this hockey game, and please make sure none of these fine athletes get hurt, and to the glory of God, amen. The puck was dropped, and four seconds later the five Birmingham guys grabbed the five Cincinnati guys and a tremendous brawl started. It was hilarious. Right after the minister extolled harmony and the glory of God, Birmingham attacked.

That's how they played. Birmingham gathered all the goons they could find and put them on the team. That brawl set the tone for the night. In the paper the next day, the headline was "Saint Valentine's Day Massacre."

That style worked great in Birmingham. The southern fans loved it. The goons became cult figures. The southern racetrack fans were looking for crashes when they came to a hockey game, just like they did in NASCAR, and that's what they got.

Cincinnati might have been a young team, but it was experienced. I wasn't playing much that first season. They sent me to the American league for about a month to get ice time. Cincinnati didn't own a team in the American league, so I went to Springfield, Massachussets. Cincinnati called it being loaned out.

That was a depressing time. I *felt* like I was being loaned out. Call it what you will, I'd been sent down to the minors. I thought my world was coming to an end. I had decided to go to Cincinnati because I thought I'd be playing there. I'd rejected the Montreal Canadiens' offer because I was sure they'd send me to play in the minors, and now here I was, sent off to play in the AHL.

I drove from Cincinnati to Springfield. I was still new to the United States, so I was driving across a strange land in the night with directions scribbled on a piece of paper. Another guy was sent down with me, Danny Justice. That helped, having another guy with me. I wasn't married, thank God. It was just me. I had just bought a car, and now it was loaded with our clothes and equipment. That would never happen today, driving to where you had been sent down. But it was different then. The two of us jumped in my car and set out for Springfield.

At that time, I thought it was the longest trip in the world. It was fifteen hours. I've done it many times since then, driving from my wife's family home in Cincinnati to our home in Glens Falls, New York. It's not that bad a trip. But that night, I was driving into what felt like oblivion, having just been sent to the minors – a twenty-year-old kid, new to the United States, with his promising hockey career seemingly in shambles.

Had I outsmarted myself by refusing the NHL and Montreal's offer? Was it over for me? I really didn't know what to think. I was going to some strange place I'd never been before. Look at it the other way round. Imagine a kid my age from Springfield being sent to Saskatchewan, driving across southern Canada in the night. Being young, good, confident, and ready to tear up the league, you don't ever think you are going to go to the minors.

For fifteen hours in the car I was rehashing my decision to go to Cincinnati, over and over. Was that the worst decision I've ever made? Would I ever get back to Cincinnati? I did find out later that Springfield would turn out to be one of the great franchises in the league, and being sent there turned out to be good for me. But that night, Springfield was a desolate place, a bleak New England town. To make it even worse, we had been booked into a terrible hotel. It was called the Wagon Wheel, and it was a rundown motel, not a hotel. Springfield was a working-class city that was undergoing tough times in the 1970s. Danny and I didn't even have our own rooms; we had to share. That motel was the icing on the lousy cake of being sent down.

As a small-town sports hero with parents, relatives, and friends who were supporting me, pushing me, and patting me on the back all the time, it was hard not to come out of Kelvington feeling like a hotshot. And obviously, coming from Canada, I was prejudiced about Canadians being by far the best hockey players. All of a sudden, I started meeting these American kids who were really good hockey players, and I started meeting Canadian kids who had been through the American college system and who were really good hockey players. That opened my eyes.

I learned that there are a lot of great players in the American Hockey League. I learned that if I intended to stay in Cincinnati, or the NHL, I was going to have to work very hard because there were a lot of guys just as good as me that could take my job.

Being sent to Springfield opened my eyes to the sobering fact that I wasn't anything special. It was good for me. It taught me what it would take to become a professional. It taught me that I had to be in shape, that I had to be ready mentally, that I had to be ready physically, that I always had to be at the top of my game. You can't take weeks off, you can't take nights off, you can't even take a shift off. Lessons like that not only made me a better player, they made me a better coach when I got into coaching.

A guy like me could not have a bad practice. I almost got to that point where I had to be one of the best practice players, because players like me cannot give the coach reasons not to like me.

What I've learned in this game is that some of the things that happen that you think are the worst possible things can turn out to be the best possible things. At the time, that month in Springfield was a tough month, a really tough month before I got the call to return to Cincinnati. But it turned out to be for the best. One of the upsides was meeting some of the young Flyers players.

In those days, Springfield was affiliated with Washington and Philadelphia. It was a poor team. It didn't make the playoffs that year. But while I was playing down there, I got to meet players from both the Capitals and the Flyers.

First of all, everybody would love to have played for the Flyers. Their building was always full, the city was hockey crazy, the team had national prominence, and there was a little self-preservation in there as well: if you played for the Flyers, it meant you didn't have to play *against* the Flyers. It would have also been nice to have been the toughest kid on the block for a while. They were winning Stanley Cups and, whether it was good or bad, they were on the national news every night. They were the big dogs, so for that reason alone, Philadelphia would have been a great place to play.

That was all on the surface. Everyone knew those things. But the Flyers were just as good behind the scenes. When I got to know several of the young Flyer guys who were playing in Springfield, they all talked about how great the organization was, how well the players were treated. They said it was a first-class organization, a great place to play.

———

In the WHA, there were a lot of teams coming and going. A team would come in for a year or two and then fold. The solid teams lasted until the merger with the NHL. Those were Edmonton, Quebec, Winnipeg, and Hartford. Cincinnati was strong, with good owners (the people who owned the Reds owned the Stingers), and so was Birmingham, who were owned by a wealthy gentleman from Toronto (they had been the Toronto Toros at one time). But neither team was considered to be in a strong enough market to survive the merger.

There was a lot of movement, shifting of teams during WHA days. Phoenix, San Diego, Denver, Indianapolis, Birmingham, Ottawa – all of them were in the WHA at some point. There were a lot of stories. Denver flew out one day for a game as the Denver Spurs, and when they landed, they were the Ottawa Nationals. They changed names in the air.

Every year, there would be players in the NHL coming to WHA, and players from the WHA going to the NHL. Every year, there would be rumours of the two leagues merging. Later on, instead of established stars, the WHA went after the young players, signing the elite players out of junior hockey before the NHL could draft them. The last year I was in Cincinnati, we had Mike Gartner and Mark Messier on the team. Gartner was eighteen years old at the time. He went on to make the Hockey Hall of Fame, with 708 goals and 627 assists in his nineteen-year NHL career, along with twenty-seven goals and twenty-five assists in the WHA. Messier, who turned pro in the WHA before his eighteenth birthday, also ended up in the Hall of Fame after playing many years as captain of the New York Rangers. He ended up with 694 goals and a whopping 1,193 assists in twenty-five NHL seasons.

At the time, I thought Gartner was going to be way better than Messier. You could tell Gartner was special. He was polished, while Mark was just a big, strong kid. But they both ended up great. It was an important lesson for me about judging talent. You shouldn't judge young players too quickly because they lack maturity. When I became a coach in junior hockey and had to make judgments about thirteen- and fourteen-year-old kids, I always kept that Gartner/Messier comparison in the back of my mind.

Birmingham had five teenagers. Edmonton had Wayne Gretzky. The signing of these young players by the WHA was one of the things that caused another change in hockey. Before the WHA came along, players weren't drafted by the NHL until they were nineteen years old. The WHA realized it was legal for kids to work at eighteen, so they started grabbing them then. With every WHA team sporting a bunch of young kids, the NHL had to change its way of doing things to stop losing the young talent. That made the NHL very angry. They'd had it their way for a long time. They didn't want to change anything.

By its last year, the WHA was a very good league. The money had kept getting better. Hockey players owe the WHA a lot, because suddenly we had leverage. If you didn't like what the NHL was offering, you had an option to go where you would probably get twice as much money, maybe even more. The NHL grew more and more furious about the increasing salaries. That's why, when the two leagues merged, NHL owners took a hard line on the WHA teams. They only let them keep two players per team, and made it very difficult for WHA teams to enter the NHL.

What gave the NHL all the cards, all the leverage to dictate the rules of the merger, was that the WHA owners wanted to belong to the bigger league so badly that they would agree to anything. Because of that, they made a deal with the devil. The WHA had done well, but the only reason you form a rival league is to create pressure that will eventually open the door to the established league. Can you imagine a team being allowed to keep only two players? It was an awful deal.

Not only that, but the rights to all the players on those four teams – except the two they kept – reverted back to the NHL teams that originally owned them. The NHL teams not only got money from each of the four teams, sort of like an admission fee to the league, they also got all their great young players back. Those WHA owners sold their teams' souls to get into the NHL.

The reserve clause got broken, too, but that was more because of baseball. In the NHL, when your contract was up, you still belonged to that team. There wasn't any free agency. You could go to the WHA, but you still weren't a free agent. If you belonged to Montreal and you had a three-year deal, even when your contract was up you couldn't go to another NHL team. You couldn't switch teams, but you could switch leagues. That's what the WHA had provided. Finally, players had some leverage, thanks to the competition. But that would come to an end.

The NHL owners were pissed at WHA because the "upstart" league had cost them a lot of money. Until then, NHL owners had a cozy little system going. They alone could determine how many teams there were, and how many markets. All the buildings were full, there were all these players eager to play, and owners had the comfort of knowing that once they drafted a kid, they owned him for life. Talk about slavery. The owners paid players what *they* wanted. The players had no alternatives. It was a great system for the NHL.

NHL owners didn't really want to merge with the WHA, but it was costing them so much money they were forced to agree to it in 1979. But they absolutely got their pound of flesh from those teams that did come into the NHL.

Cincinnati had good teams. We never won a championship, but we made the playoffs two out of three years. It was a well-run organization with stable ownership. Our owners were as wealthy as any in the WHA. We had a beautiful building, and had 12,000 fans most nights, sometimes as many as 14,000 or 15,000. We were drawing as well as a lot of the NHL teams. Madison Square Garden holds 18,000 for hockey. A lot of the new buildings seat 20,000. But in the '70s, an arena that held 16,000 to 17,000 for hockey was a big building.

I met my wife in Cincinnati in 1977, not long after I returned from Springfield. The Stingers were one of the first hockey teams to have cheerleaders. Carpets would be placed on the ice during intermissions, and the girls would dance and do their routines. They were called the Honeybees. One day, the team had a meet-and-greet event for VIPs and season-ticket holders. A bunch of players were there, me included, along with a bunch of the Honeybees. Afterwards, my buddy Dennis Abgrall and I were walking to our cars and met two of the Honeybees. We said hello, introduced ourselves, and talked for a few minutes. I was quite taken by one of the girls.

There was a game the next night, and there were the

Honeybees. I picked out the girls we'd met in the parking lot, and I remembered their names, but I wasn't sure which name belonged to which girl. So I got hold of Chuck Stout, one of our stick boys who helped out around the dressing room and lugged equipment to the bench. I opened the game program to the Honeybees' picture, pointed out the girl I had met, and told Chuck he had to go upstairs and get her phone number. So he went up and got Cindy's phone number, and I called and asked her out.

The Stingers eventually enacted a rule that said the players couldn't date Honeybees, but that was after Cindy and I had been living together. We were married in 1978, and we've been together since.

For the most part, I stayed healthy. My worst injury was a shoulder separation my second year with the Stingers. I was chasing the puck into the corner with this big guy on my tail. His name was Peter Driscoll. He hit me into the glass. It was a strong hit, but clean. My shoulder hit the glass at a funny angle and my arm popped out of the socket. It was a freak injury.

It was one of the worst pains I've ever felt in my life. It kept me out of the lineup for about a month, because after they put your arm back in the socket, you have to wait for it to heal. Then you go about regaining your strength with exercises. But until it heals, you can't do *anything* with your arm but rest it. You can't lift it, or even move it very much.

Separated shoulders can get worse. I know guys you could slap on the shoulder and their arm would pop out. That's when you have to have surgery where they cut the tendons, shorten them, and tie them back together. You do not want to get to that point. But once you've had a separated shoulder, the next one happens more easily.

Other than that, I stayed healthy. Each year, I played more and more. By the third year, I was a solid, reliable player. The first year, I had been intimidated a little by the size of the guys I was playing with. Looking back, I should have been more confident, more aggressive, because I was big enough at six foot two and 220 pounds. By the third year, I had gotten it together and was more of a physical presence. I think I was one of the better defencemen in the WHA. The proof was that the Cincinnati front office came to me and wanted to renegotiate my contract for another two years. If the WHA had kept going, I would have been in great shape. That made me feel I was on my way to becoming a solid professional.

5

Barry and the Jets

Every summer, I'd go back to Kelvington and work on the farm. I'd be on the tractor, sometimes twenty hours a day. I've farmed with my dad and grandfather since I was a kid. Farming was going to be my retirement. I'd play hockey as long as I could, then go back and farm in Saskatchewan. Plus, we had a really good baseball team in Kelvington. All the local professional hockey players would come home in the summer. Every baseball team had hockey players on the roster. We'd work all week, have baseball practice after work, and play games on the weekends. Wendel Clark, Joey Kocur, Trent Yawney, Kelly Chase, Kevin Kaminski were all in the NHL and they all played baseball with me in the summer. People came from all over to watch us play. If you look at an NHL contract, there's a lot of stuff you are not allowed to do, but playing baseball isn't one of them.

After the 1978-79 season, I had signed a new contract. I was happy where I was. I would have been happy playing in

Cincinnati the rest of my life. There were rumours about a merger with the NHL, but those rumours had been in the air for three years. I was too busy to worry much about it.

That summer, the rumours came true. Four WHA teams merged with the NHL. Birmingham and Cincinnati were the two that didn't. I wasn't too worried. I knew I was going to be playing *someplace* the following year. I just had no idea where.

As soon as the merger took place, I became the property of the Montreal Canadiens. I expected them to trade me, but I really didn't know. I was never the type to worry about where I ended up. There aren't many places that are going to have worse weather than Saskatchewan. It's not like I grew up in Miami. Anyplace was fine with me. As long as I was being paid to play hockey, I was the happiest guy in the world.

I never even met with Montreal. The four WHA teams met around the table with the NHL, and deals got hammered out. They had a draft, and Montreal traded my rights to the Winnipeg Jets. It all happened behind the scenes.

Four of us from Cincinnati – Craig Norwich, Peter Marsh, Barry Legge, and myself – ended up belonging to the Winnipeg Jets. I finally found out where I was going through John Ferguson, the GM of the Jets. He called me a couple of days before the draft and told me Winnipeg was going to acquire my rights. I knew Winnipeg well – it was close to Kelvington, a good hockey city.

John Ferguson flew me and a couple of other guys into Montreal so we would be on hand to meet the press. I was actually there when the draft was taking place. Not that I had any say about it. Hockey players had no say about their destiny in my era. We went where we were told, and were hopeful that we'd get a decent contract for what we were doing.

We could try to negotiate if we thought we needed a better deal, but they could also tell us to f-off. And it wasn't like there was any other place to go. The WHA was gone. Players had no leverage – once again. Winnipeg owned my rights. I was either going to play there, or quit. So I signed a contract with them.

As it happened, the Jets were great. They treated me fairly. Looking back, what we were paid was a joke compared to what players get now. But at the time it seemed okay. My first year with the Jets, I made sixty-thousand dollars. The average NHL salary is $2 million today. Back then, we had no idea what other players made. Keeping us in the dark was just another way the owners kept their feet on players' necks. If the best defenceman in the league didn't know he was only the tenth-best-paid defenceman, he couldn't negotiate a better deal for himself based on that. Players didn't exchange salary information because our agents told us not to. For some crazy reason, we thought it made sense to keep our salaries private. That's how stupid we were. Things have changed. Every contract is public now because of the players' association and the salary cap. But as I have said, I was being paid to *play hockey,* and that was good.

I knew a lot of guys on the Jets. The team had a lot of WHA guys. There were the four guys from Cincinnati who went with me, and I had played against most of the other guys who were on the team. By now, I had experience moving into a new territory, having done it in Kamloops and Cincinnati. You get used to meeting new teammates and making new friends. It's part of the life of a professional athlete.

Scotty Campbell was one of the two players the Jets kept from their WHA roster. When he had played for Houston and Winnipeg in the WHA, Campbell and I must have had ten fights a year. Our first meeting as teammates was on the team bus. I had stepped on board, and there was Scotty. We looked at each other and started laughing. One of the guys from the previous year's Winnipeg team said, "You guys are going to be okay sitting on the bus together, aren't you?" That broke the ice. Everybody had a good laugh. We became good teammates. That sort of thing happens in all sports. And with hockey, fighting is just part of the job.

I played two years with the Jets. We were never very good because the NHL had taken so many players during the merger. It was a tough year on the ice. We weren't very talented. There weren't a lot of wins in Winnipeg. I assisted on the first Winnipeg goal ever scored, so that's always in the record books.

Tommy McVie was our coach. He's one of the most famous guys in hockey. He's one of those classic coaches who has been in hockey his whole life. He's coached every minor league team in the world, and also worked for a bunch of NHL teams, either as coach or a scout. In fact, he just got his name engraved on the Stanley Cup in 2011 as a member of the Boston Bruins organization, after almost forty years in hockey.

Tommy is one of the funniest guys I ever met, a real character. In the '80s, Clint Eastwood made a movie called *Heartbreak Ridge*. Clint's character was a hard-fighting, hard-drinking sergeant in the marines, a Medal of Honor–winner who was training young marines. Had a really gravelly voice. He had a great speech in the movie. He lined up his frightened recruits and got in their faces, spitting at them through clenched teeth: "Don't think you guys can surprise me, I've done everything you've done and then some. I've drunk more beer, I've had more women, I've been in more fights, killed more gooks. . . ." It's a wonderful speech. Intense. Tommy used to give that same exact speech. Of course, Tommy's came long before Clint's. When he would get his team together for the first time, he'd start this long rant about how there's nothing the team can do that will surprise him, he's been there and done that – more beer, more broads, more fights – on and on, only Tommy's got the deepest voice in the world and he seems to go on forever without taking a breath. He sounds just like a marine sergeant.

It's one of the greatest speeches I ever heard from a coach or anybody else. The first time I heard it, I was sitting there thinking, "I'm playing for this caricature of every coach I ever heard of all clumped into one guy." Everyone who's played for Tommy, whether it was in the '70s, '80, or '90s, has heard that speech. We can all pretty much recite it – at least, we always try when we get together.

One night in Philly, five or six of us went out for a few beers. We didn't have curfew, so we came in around one a.m. The guy at the desk asked if we were with the Winnipeg Jets, and we said yeah. He said he had our sandwiches ready. We didn't know what he was talking about. He said, "The sandwiches Mr. McVie ordered are at the desk here. You guys can take them if you want." We went to the end of the desk, and there was this beautiful tray of sandwiches. We were starved.

We looked at each other, and the light bulb went on: "Let's take Tommy's sandwiches." We thought it would be funny.

The next morning, we came down to get on the bus, and Tommy was in a rage in the lobby, pacing around and ranting. He waited until we were all on the bus, and he got on and said, in that gravely bass voice of his, "Okay, which one of you bastards ate my fockin' sandwiches?!" I'd never seen him so mad. He had gotten back later than us, and because he was smarter than we were, like he said in his famous speech, he had ordered sand-wiches to have before he went to bed. Like he told us, he'd been there. He knew if you're going to stay out late drinking beer, you should think ahead and have sandwiches ready at the desk.

We were like schoolboys. We didn't know if we should tell him we took the sandwiches. Finally, Jude Drouin, who'd played in the NHL for the New York Islanders and Minnesota, put his hand up and said, "Tommy, I took your sandwiches. Five of us came in late, we didn't know you wanted them that badly, we thought it would be funny." He never did give the rest of us up. Jude took all the blame. I'll always think fondly of Jude Drouin for not giving up the rest of us.

Tommy was a physical fitness nut. I know we worked harder than any other team in the NHL. He said we might not be the best team, but we'd be the fittest. We had frequent weigh-ins, and we had to either make our weight or find a way to lose some pounds. We had circuit training. Teams used to come watch us practise and shake their heads. They couldn't believe how hard we worked. I was in my best shape ever when I was playing for Tommy.

There were some tough times. I got my jaw busted the first

year with Winnipeg. I took an elbow from my own teammate. I was chasing a guy into the corner, and my teammate came down from the point to hit the guy. He missed the guy and hit me. His elbow busted my jaw in three places, knocked out all my teeth. They took me from the dressing room to the dentist's chair – with my equipment still on – and I was there until four in the morning.

It was a tough injury to get over, but I only ended up missing three games. They wired my jaw back together and gave me a form-fitting mask to wear over my face. It was a skin-tight mask made of fibreglass. If I got hit in the face, it would spread the impact of the blow. I looked like Hannibal Lecter, but it worked. I got hit a few times with the mask on. I felt it. It hurt, but the mask did spread the blow out.

Even when the going got tough, either with injuries or trades, I never thought about doing anything but playing hockey. I started getting paid to play hockey when I was fifteen. From that moment on, I knew there was not another thing in the world I wanted to do. I used to go home and work on the farm in the off-season, so I knew that there was a real world out there, and it wasn't for me. I realized that I was going to make a living from hockey, one way or another, for the rest of my life because hockey was what I loved.

I would often sit and have a beer with the guys and listen to them bitch about the game and how they couldn't wait to get done with hockey. All these guys had big ideas of what they were going to do when they were done playing. When I'd run into them five, ten years later, chances are they would be adrift. A lot of them did not succeed in the private world, and frankly, that was predictable. Those who did succeed hated whatever they had traded hockey for. I realized that I had a great job and I that I wanted to stay involved with the game. I was pretty lucky that way. You could say my whole life has been pretty one-dimensional, but as I said, I knew from early on that hockey would be my life. I've been very lucky it worked out.

When I played, even the wealthy guys did not have enough money to retire. The highest-paid guys in the league back then were making two to three hundred thousand dollars. When you're an athlete, you blow through your money pretty quickly because you think it's going to be there forever. I know many guys who vowed to start saving money "next year." What if, all of a sudden, your career comes to a grinding halt? You always think you'll play for another four or five years. You'll get things straightened out next month or next year, and then bang, suddenly you're done. Instead of making a hundred thousand a year, you're making nothing. It can be a rude awakening, because most of the players didn't have enough money to retire and do nothing the rest of their lives. They all had to find something to do. I am vested in the NHL pension fund – I played enough games to meet the requirements – but that's not enough to live on. A lot of guys my age decided to invest in businesses. Unfortunately, most of them just weren't good businesspeople.

A common dream of players had to do with opening a restaurant or a bar. We had all watched *Cheers,* and Sam Malone looked pretty cool. A lot of those guys got burned because that was a business they knew very little about. They'd put up the money and go in with a partner who would run the restaurant. Once you had some experience, you realized that a bar/restaurant back then was a cash business. If you're not there all the time, the cash tends to walk. That happened to several guys I knew. They would open a restaurant with a buddy, or someone who knew the restaurant business, and those guys would spend all the money. The restaurant would go under and the retired player would be left with nothing.

The older hockey players are bad at business in general. Hockey players tend to trust people too easily. We can be pretty gullible at times, especially guys who played in the '70s. That's why there were a lot of hockey players who lost a lot of money when they retired. The new guys are a lot more business savvy. They have business managers and investment advisers. They learned from the mistakes of the older guys.

Everyone was tested, all the time. You had to stand up for yourself. As I said, you had to prove to the guys on your own team that you were tough enough to go into New Westminster or Birmingham or Philadelphia or Boston and play, and not be scared. Testing was a big thing in that era. Number one, you had to prove to your own team that you had enough guts to play, but also you had to prove to the rest of the league that you weren't a coward, that you were able to play that rough style of hockey. It was much more of a physically testing league then than it is today.

The minute you were slashed or tripped, you had to either stand up and take your gloves off, or at least slash the guy back or do something to show you didn't accept that kind of treatment. In most cases, you had to fight to show the rest of the league that you were brave enough, and you weren't going to let people just give you the face wash – or slash you in the ankles or spear you – and do nothing about it.

A face wash is when you take your glove, which you've been wearing all year long – take the smelly, sweaty, stinky palm of your glove – and rub it in the other guy's face. It's a standard hockey move. More fights have been started because of the face wash than probably any other symbol of disrespect in the NHL. Slashing a guy in the ankles has started a lot of fights, too. Or say a guy drops his glove. You skate by and flip it away with your stick as he bends down to pick it up. That started a lot of fights.

Running into the other team's goaltender is a surefire fight starter. In the '70s, that started more fights than anything. Goaltenders were sacred in the NHL. If a player on another team bumped into your goalie or harassed him in any other way, the fight was on. If you needed to start a fight, that was a guaranteed way of doing it. Even if the other team did not want to fight, even if the other team had no tough guys on the team, that forced somebody to do something. You can't touch the other team's goaltender. That's a real taboo in hockey. Goaltenders are a protected species. They are like the bald eagle. They can play the puck outside the crease and cannot be touched. They are protected by the rule book, but they've also always been protected by their teammates. There's an unwritten rule that goaltenders are not to be hit outside the crease. Everybody goes by that.

———

Those years in Winnipeg were definitely not the highlight of my career. The last season was especially brutal. It caught us by surprise. I'd played well the year before, solidified my place on the team. We'd added some good young guys in the draft, and we'd gotten used to playing in the NHL the year before, so we thought we'd have a pretty good team. Not a playoff team, but a competitive team. Then it just went bad. The season started terribly. I wasn't playing well, the team wasn't jelling. It started snowballing. You could feel it.

I could have made myself a better player, but I didn't have the experience then to know how to go about changing the way I was playing. When I got older and started coaching, I realized that what Winnipeg needed from me back then was to become a solid defensive defenceman, a guy they could depend on back there, closer to my own net. That's how I could have made myself valuable and stayed with the team – worrying more about goals *against* than trying to be part *of* the offence. But I was young, and felt I had to be making big plays to impress the coaching staff, so I was joining the rush, trying to score goals and make assists.

Another thing you learn as you mature as a defenceman is never to get in foot races. Never give the forward the advantage of having a foot race with you, because he is going to win. I was guilty of doing that too much.

But the fact is, we had a bad team. The Jets, like other WHA teams, had been decimated by the impossible conditions of the merger, namely only being able to keep two players. It wasn't a fair starting point. It took all the WHA teams a lot of time to get up to speed. It took Winnipeg even longer. We were bad.

There's a saying in hockey: "You can't make chicken salad out of chicken shit." We were chicken shit.

I believe Winnipeg had a losing streak that year that came close to the NHL record of seventeen set by the Washington Capitals in 1974–75. I was out of there before then. Winnipeg decided to send me down to the minors in December. I was lucky, though: Toronto picked me up off of waivers before I even played a game in the AHL. So for me, it went from being a really rough time to being a great time, joining the team I had rooted for my whole life, the greatest team in Canada.

6

Thinking-Man's Game

After my season and a third in Winnipeg, Toronto picked me up off of waivers. Tommy McVie called to let me know I'd be coming to Toronto. That's how it's supposed to work. You hear horror stories about players being called by the trainer, or finding out what's happened in their lives from the radio or TV. The coach should be the one to call you. I vowed that when I started coaching I would always do that – I would always do the dirty jobs, like personally telling players when they were traded, cut, or sent down. I think it's important that the coach be the face or the voice a player sees or hears when he has to be given that kind of news. I always respected Tommy for telling me himself.

Floyd Smith is the reason I ended up in Toronto. Floyd had coached me in Cincinnati and had moved to Toronto as director of player personnel after the Stingers folded. He liked me when I played in Cincinnati, and I enjoyed playing for him. So when I became available, he brought me along. That's how I ended up going to my all-time favourite team, the one I grew up watching and rooting for, the Toronto Maple Leafs.

Anytime you're moved, you're shaken up a little bit. I had developed a comfort zone in Winnipeg. But a chance to play for the Toronto Maple Leafs is something that Canadian kids dream about their whole lives. Going to Toronto was like a ballplayer going to the New York Yankees, or a football player going to the Green Bay Packers. Wearing a Toronto major league hockey jersey is pretty special.

I remember I flew into Toronto. Back then, you carried your own equipment, so I was lugging my equipment with me in addition to my baggage. The team had me picked up at the airport and taken to a hotel that was right next door to Maple Leaf Gardens. I spent a nervous night there. The next morning, I got up and walked over to the Gardens with my gear. It was a nervous morning. I didn't know many Toronto players. After a while, you know players on just about every team, but for some reason that wasn't the case with Toronto. Usually, there is someone you played with in junior hockey, the AHL, or the NHL on a team you join, but there wasn't one guy in the dressing room I knew.

Not only was it a new team with a lot of strange faces, but it was *the* Toronto Maple Leafs. I met the guys at the morning skate, pulled on the blue and white Toronto jersey for the first time, found my locker, and got acquainted with the Toronto dressing room.

In hockey, a new team doesn't mean a new playbook or a new system. Teams today have a few special things they do on power plays, or when clearing the puck, but even now the game is not highly scripted. That's what makes hockey players different from other athletes. Baseball, for example, is very organized. It's a game of statistics and percentages. Defensive field positioning is called from the dugout because of computer databases that crunch records and predict where batters are likely to hit. Runners are given signs when managers want them to steal. Pitches are called from the bench. Batters get signals telling them to take, hit away, bunt, or hit and run.

Hockey, on the other hand, is a game of reacting. There are concepts for breakouts (starting an attack from deep in your own end) and a few other things, but really, the vast majority of hockey teams – in those days, especially – played the same way. You forechecked with two men, with a third guy high. The defencemen's responsibilities were the same.

Everyone on the ice is a role player. All eighteen skaters on the team have something particular they contribute. There are defensive defencemen, who are the shutdown guys. They are usually pretty good skaters, and they are strong, very defensive minded. They know what they are there for, so they don't take risks on offence. The Washington Capitals' Rod Langway is a good example. He's won the Norris Trophy as the league's best defenceman. Another is Tim Horton, who played for Toronto, Buffalo, and other teams – the defenceman I idolized as a kid. And, of course, Rob Blake, who played for me in Los Angeles. Current heavies on defence are Zdeno Chara of Boston and the New York Rangers' Dan Girardi.

Offensive defencemen are faster, quicker. They'll skate the puck out of the defensive zone, and run the power play from the point. Those guys usually have wicked shots, like Detroit's Reed Larson, who had the hardest shot I've ever seen. Al Iafrate, who was mostly with the Leafs and Washington Capitals in the 1980s and '90s, was an amazing athlete who also had a shot over a hundred miles an hour – and he used a wooden stick. And Doug Wilson of the Chicago Blackhawks was an excellent offensive defenceman. Today's standouts are Florida's Brian Campbell, Ottawa's Erik Karlsson, and Nashville's Shea Weber.

The forecheckers go in and lay on big hits. They are fast, single-minded message senders. They know their role is to go in and drill people, finish every check. Good examples are Terry O'Reilly, who played fourteen seasons with the Boston Bruins, and Bob Gainey, who played sixteen years with Montreal. John Tonelli, who played for the Islanders, Calgary, and Los Angeles, was a great forechecker, as was Brian Sutter, who played for St. Louis. In the 1990s, Wendel Clark was probably the best forechecker in the NHL. Today's standouts are Ryan Kesler (Vancouver) and Milan Lucic (Boston).

Checking, delivering solid hits, is a key element of our game. It also happens to be one of those elements that requires good timing, because there is only a split second between a good check and a penalty. Hit a man without the puck, and it is interference. But if he has the puck, and you have started your check, you can usually finish it without getting a call – even if he gets rid of the puck before you hit him. We had a guideline when I was coaching. I'd tell my players if they were within a stick-length of the guy with the puck, finish the check. You won't get called for interference if you are that close. Interference was rarely called in the old days. Nowadays, the

NHL has adopted a tougher policy about calling interference.

The skill guys are the best skaters, thinkers, and reactors on the ice. They are the most creative guys. Their job is to either score goals or set people up to score. They are great passers. Adam Oates, who played for seven different NHL teams, is a good example. He scored 341 goals in his career, but had 1,079 assists. And Wayne Gretzky, of course. Gretzky always thought "pass" before he thought "shoot." Always. Gretzky scored 894 goals in his NHL career, and had 1,963 assists.

There are the fighters, guys like Chicago's Behn Wilson and Keith Magnuson, Bob Gassoff of St. Louis, and me. I had to fight and hit to stay in the NHL. We all did. Some fighters logged as many as five hundred penalty minutes in one season. My average was one hundred and fifty minutes a season. My career total was just over seven hundred.

To say that goalies are "different" isn't a strong enough word. They are weird guys. Goalies are very different cats. The football guys say the punters and kickers are the crazy ones in their sport. In hockey, it's the goalies. They can be really good, like Kelly Hrudey, who played for me in Los Angeles. Kelly was one of the greatest competitors I ever knew, a guy I loved to coach. Even Kelly was on the weird side, but in a productive way.

I'm a guy who sets goals. I write my goals in a little book. They range from one to ten years in the future. Probably because of that, I have read a lot of Tony Robbins, a motivational guru who has designed systems for realizing your goals. When I got to the NHL, I wrote to Robbins, saying that meeting him was one of my goals. He wrote back and we met, became friends. I asked Tony to come speak to the team, and I introduced him to Kelly, who was really struggling. Kelly had told me he had lost confidence. So I asked him if he'd be open to meeting Tony Robbins and talking with him. He said he'd try anything.

That's what I mean by Kelly being weird. No other goalie I ever met would have done that. Most hockey players I know wouldn't have done it. It's very hard to get athletes to try something that isn't mainstream. In general, we really are a superstitious bunch. But Kelly would try stuff. He was open, not scared of making a fool of himself. He jumped in. Working with Tony Robbins changed him, gave him some great exercises to do when he doubted himself and found his confidence lacking. He played great the rest of the year, and we went on to the Stanley Cup finals.

Goalies are probably more stable in today's hockey world, thanks to huge improvements in protective padding, but the guys I played with, and the ones before that, were truly nuts. To begin with, it takes a certain type of guy to want to play that position. If you think it's fun to have twenty of your best friends get together to shoot a couple of hundred pucks at you at a hundred miles an hour, you can't be all there. That happens at team practice almost every day for ten months a year.

The number of shots a goalie faces in practice is crazy. And goalies have to do all the drills the rest of the team does. And those heavy pads look big, but in my day they didn't offer a ton of protection. Goalies are bruised and battered all the time. That goes with the job. You've got to be a bit touched just to want to play that position.

Added to all the physical pressure on a goalie, there's also the emotional stuff. If the goalie allows a soft goal late in the game, he gets blamed. If a forward makes a mistake that results in giving up the winning goal, it's no big deal. It probably won't even be in the highlight reel. But if a goalie lets in a softie, that *is* the highlight. It takes a certain type of guy to handle that sort of pressure.

All of them handle it differently. There are stories about Ed Belfour, who played for Toronto, Dallas, and Chicago. On a game day, Belfour refused to talk with other guys on the team. He'd stay within himself, locked up in his world. That was Belfour's way. Marty Brodeur, the New Jersey Devils' great goalie, would talk his pants off until game time. He wouldn't shut up. Hall of Famer Glenn Hall, who played over nine hundred games, used to throw up before every one. Some goalies talk a blue streak when they are playing. Some of them are dicks on the day of a game. They all handle it differently.

Goalie equipment is much, much better now. But you can still take shots off the inside of your leg, or off your toe, or get hit in the back of your hand. You still get popped quite a bit, even with equipment that is a thousand times better than it was in the '70s and '80s. Fifty years ago, goalies didn't even wear masks. If they've got to be nuts to play today with proper equipment, how would you rate one of those guys being in goal without a mask? Goalies were much crazier in the old days.

We have a hockey tradition in Canada. When your kids are toddlers, you give them an IQ test. If your kid is really smart, you make him a defenceman; if the kid is just average, you make him a forward; and if the kid flunks the test, you put him in net.

In all seriousness, defence *is* the hardest position to play. You have to react to what the other team's forwards are doing, and to react to what your own forwards are doing. You have to ask yourself, "Does it look like your guys are going to get into the offensive zone? Do they have a good angle on the other guys?" And half the time, you're doing everything while skating backwards.

Forwards don't need to do nearly as much thinking as defencemen. Forwards carry the puck in and attack. Granted, they have to be great skaters, they need great hand–eye coordination, and they have to do magical things with the puck. Not to mention they need to have a great shot. But they are free spirits. To be a good defenceman, you have to be a thinker. You've got to read and react, and adjust and monitor your play to what the other team is doing. I think most forwards would agree.

Forwards have a lot more freedom than defencemen. If a defenceman continues into the offensive play and no one backs him up, there could be an odd-man rush, a two-on-one the other way. The forward should back him up, but maybe he doesn't. Before a defenceman goes into the play, he has to look to make sure a forward is backing him up. Defence is the toughest position to play in hockey.

While everybody on the ice knows his job, his role, there's no master plan for putting it all together. When the puck drops, everyone does his job in the most imaginative way possible. As soon as you attack, the other team reacts. They've watched you play. They more or less know what your breakout scheme is and what you like to do. When you have a two-on-one break, you have a million options. The defender reacts to what you are doing, tries to stop your attack. What's the guy in the middle going to do – shoot, or pass? Will the guy on the outside curl and drag the puck into the middle, then drop a pass, or will he shoot? The defenceman reacts, and then you have to react to his reaction. It's the same when it's five-on-five, four-on-four, three-on-two, whatever. The options are endless.

A hockey player has to be thinking all the time. There aren't spots on the ice you just go to in given situations. In a football play, everyone on the field knows exactly where he is going. Every play has been diagrammed. There's very little innovation or imagination *during* a play, unless it's broken and the quarterback has to scramble. But if a receiver uses his imagination to begin with, the play will be broken because the quarterback is throwing to a particular spot, and the receiver had better be in that spot.

Hockey is entirely different. The team that reacts the best, thinks the fastest, creates the most opportunities, and most successfully coordinates its collective imagination is the team that wins, that has great players.

Wayne Gretzky was one of hockey's greatest thinkers and reactors. Gretz always thought ahead of the play, most definitely. When I coached him, he would do something during a game, and sometimes I would look at what he did and question it. After his shift, I'd ask him, "Why were you there? You should have been here." And he'd say he just had a feeling that the puck was going to be there. Nine times out of ten, he'd be right.

Gretzky had great imagination and creativity. He did things and tried things that no one else had ever thought of. He's the one who started coming from behind the opposing team's net to score goals. He pretty much invented the wraparound. He got a lot of his goals that way.

The great players change the game. Bobby Orr made hockey different. Defencemen never used to cross the other team's blue line. Defencemen used to get two or three goals a year. Defencemen always passed the puck out of their zone. If they did carry the puck out, they stopped as soon as they got to centre ice. Not Bobby Orr. He led the rush and loved scoring goals. He even won the scoring race twice in his career. He scored forty-six goals one season. He completely changed the game in the '70s. And then Gretzky came in and changed it again in the '80s.

Aside from reinventing the way goals were scored, Gretzky was amazing at avoiding hits. I've only seen him get hit twice in his career. First of all, he was always protected by his team. When Wayne played for Edmonton, there was a tough guy named Dave Semenko who protected him. Every team Gretzky was with always had a tough guy assigned to him. When I had him in L.A., it was Marty McSorley. Gretz always knew someone had his back. The opposition also knew, and because of that, no one took licence with Gretzky. Guys knew if they did something nasty to Gretz, they were going to have to pay a heavy price.

Gretzky was smarter than everyone else, another reason he rarely got hit. Of the two times I saw him hit, one was legal. The other was a dirty hit from behind. Usually, Gretzky had eyes in the back of his head. He could see the entire ice. And he never skated with his head down. You never got an open lick at him. He had longevity because he never put himself in a position to get drilled.

That's what I mean when I say hockey is a game of reaction. There's never a playbook that stipulates when I go here, you go there. It doesn't work like that. From start to finish, you are thinking, trying to stay a step ahead of the opposition. They're trying to stay a step ahead of you.

There's one other aspect that's very critical with every hockey team: the dressing room. There are guys on every team who are known as "good in the room." A team cannot get along without those guys, because they keep the dressing room loose and happy.

A hockey dressing room is one of my favourite places in the world. I love the dressing room. You've got nineteen of your good friends in there. You're all laughing and joking and telling stories. It's funny, but the language and some of the things that are said would shock most people. It's very male-oriented, a very tight group.

We use this phrase liberally, and we don't mean it literally, but you and your teammates "go to war." You're fighting together, travelling together, you're playing tired, sick, and hurt together. I hear stories about soldiers who put their lives on the line for each other, and how close they are. I can relate that to hockey players. I know how bonded we become because of what we go through.

The dressing room is where you can say to each other, "Wow, we made it through another game against Philadelphia or Boston without losing our heads." It's like that. You're telling stories, you're telling jokes. Every team has its comedians. Every team has three or four guys who are a little nerdy. They're a little different, so they create lots of stories and situations that everybody shares. They get practical jokes played on them. And the single guys are telling stories about what is going on in their lives. The dressing room is hilarious at times. It's a true fraternity.

Humour is key in the dressing room. It's the best outlet for stress. That's why you see guys laying it on each other and playing practical jokes right up to game time, because humour takes the edge off, takes the pressure off, loosens everyone up.

Once, during a practice in Toronto, guys from the front office showed up and took one of our players off the ice because he had been traded. It was trade-deadline time, and that happens, but it put everyone on edge. Guys started looking over their shoulders. We got into the dressing room, and one of our right wingers, Ricky Vaive, came over, tapped me on the shoulder, and whispered that Mike Nykoluk, our coach, wanted to see me. Ricky was really solemn-faced about it. I thought, "Oh jeez, here it comes. I'm either going to be sent down or traded." I made the walk of shame to Mike's office with everyone watching. I knocked, poked my head in, and said, "You wanted to see me?" Mike, a former player, looked at me and started laughing. He said, "Barry, someone is pulling your chain."

I turned around, walked back, and there were nineteen guys laughing their asses off. So, of course, I took off after Ricky Vaive. I was usually the one getting guys, but they got me good that day.

When you're in junior hockey, the company in the dressing room is all guys from western Canada. Then you become a pro, and the players are from all over the world. The foreign players add something to the dynamic. A dressing room is different now than it was twenty or thirty years ago because of the Europeans, Russians, and Nordic guys. Their language, their accents, their various versions of English open up a whole new raft of jokes and situations. The foreign players help make it all more interesting.

And yes, it is a crude place. A lot of things are said in the dressing room that would embarrass most people. You've got twenty athletes walking around naked a lot of the time. Everyone is ripping everyone else, criticizing everybody else's manliness. You have to be sharp in the dressing room. When I was with Toronto, Billy Derlago, one of my teammates, would often come walking up to me naked after the game and ask me if I'd seen his beer. I knew what was coming. He did it all the time. I'd just smile and say no, I hadn't seen his beer. He'd turn around and walk away, and he'd have the beer can wedged in the crack of his butt.

You've got to have a good sense of humour. And you've got to have a solid belief in yourself, because otherwise you can be brought down in the dressing room very quickly. It's a haven for bullshit. It's also a great leveller, a place to let it all hang out and come to terms with it. You literally can't conceal anything in the dressing room. When you've been with a bunch of guys every day for a year, and you know how everyone reacts under stress and intimidation, you find out a lot about them. You also find out a lot about yourself.

For players, the dressing room teaches, and helps promote, survival. For a perceptive coach, the dressing room is a human resources lab where he watches what happens in various situations, and learns volumes about his team.

The first game I played with Toronto was probably the most nervous I've ever been in my whole life. It was against Pittsburgh.

They put me in the starting lineup. After the national anthems, I was almost shaking with nerves. There I was in Toronto, on the ice at Maple Leaf Gardens, one of hockey's biggest stages. I had been watching this team play since 1960. It was always my favourite team, and now I was on it. *Whew!*

I was in such a state that I knew I had to do something, but I had no idea what. No more than seven or eight seconds into the game, I grabbed a guy and got in a fight. I didn't plan it, I just did it – grabbed this guy and went into the corner with him, where we had a quick fight. That got me settled down and ready to play.

I had a great game. I played well, and even got a shorthanded goal. We won the game. The thing I remember about this game – and it was a good indication of what playing in Toronto was like – is that there I was, the new guy. I got in a fight, scored a shorthanded goal, but still, in the third period, some fan stood up behind the bench and yelled, "Hey, Melrose, what are you gonna do tonight?" I couldn't believe my ears. One of my teammates, a large, tough guy named Dan Maloney, stood up on the bench, turned around, and told the guy to shut his mouth or he was going to come up there and kick his ass.

From that moment on, Dan Maloney was one of my favourite guys. He turned out to be one of the best teammates I ever played with in my life, and he became one of my best friends.

A hockey team is like any business. You have a boss, and there's the front office, with all its bureaucratic hierarchy, complexities, rules, relationships, and politics. And there is your group of workers, your teammates. Management likes certain players, doesn't like others. Some guys get on with the system, some don't. But the good thing about hockey is you make friends very quickly. Each time you move, it gets easier.

I moved to Weyburn, then on to Kamloops, Cincinnati, and Winnipeg. The person this is hardest on is your wife. Once you start moving with a wife and family, everything gets doubly difficult, because you're bringing your kids into it too, and that means changing schools, separation from friends. I was lucky. My wife, Cindy, is very outgoing and gregarious. Moving was never a big problem for us, but it was for a lot of other players who had families.

Playing professional hockey is like life in the military. You hear all these stories about guys like Ray Bourque and Stevie Yzerman playing with the same team for twenty years and how great that is. But you don't hear so much about the players who end up moving ten times in ten years. When I went on to coaching, I moved four times in five years: Medicine Hat to Seattle, Glens Falls, Los Angeles, and back to Glens Falls. I never had the luxury of staying in one place for five years, let alone twenty.

In hockey, the subculture is very strong. The expression "he's a hockey player" speaks volumes about what kind of guy that person is. Of course, every player is an individual, no two are alike, but they do have a lot in common. For the most part, hockey players are a bunch of courageous guys who have made a lifelong commitment to a very fast, physical, dangerous game. They are both physically tough and tough-minded.

Hockey players are a very macho group. You're judged by how tough you are, by how much pain you can take. Hockey players take pride in things like getting cut, going into the dressing room and needing forty stitches to close the wound and only missing a couple of shifts. Very few athletes in other sports do that sort of thing. Bicycle racers are the only athletes I can think of who continue to ride after being severely hurt in a crash.

Hockey players are also polite. They blab less to the press than athletes in other sports. But if asked, they will talk. They might not say much, but neither will they tell a reporter to f-off. Most hockey players are engaging, funny. That's how we are raised. Ask any reporter. Nine times out of ten, he'll say the hockey player is the best athlete to deal with.

The hockey universe is small. The players' universe is even smaller, and very interconnected. You get to a new team, and most often if you don't know somebody on that team, you know somebody who knows somebody. What also happens a lot is that players from certain parts of the country end up hanging out together. Western kids become friends, and eastern kids become friends because of the geography they have in common. When European players came into the mix, we all started becoming friends with them because, well, they are hockey players no matter where they learned to play the game.

My first year in Toronto, we arrived just before Christmas. Cindy and I hadn't yet found a place to live. So Dan Maloney and his wife invited Cindy and me over on Christmas Day. They had a family with young kids; we were staying in a hotel. Dan didn't have to do that, but he knew we were young and by ourselves. We went over and had a great Christmas with the Maloney family. That's how the hockey community is.

I loved Toronto, loved playing there, loved Maple Leaf Gardens, loved the emotions running rampant throughout the city about the team. It was a great time in my life. My wife and I were young, living downtown next to the Gardens. I got to play with Ronny Ellis toward the end of his career. And I got to be around guys like Johnny Bower, Bobby Baun, George Armstrong, *and* Carl Brewer – guys I'd kept track of my whole life. They had all retired, but they often came out to practice with us, and were generally on the scene. Being able to hang out with them was a treat.

Toronto and Montreal are magical places in Canada. I've been lucky. I was drafted by Montreal, played for Toronto, and played for Detroit, another Original Six team. Toronto and Montreal are still magical for Canadians.

It doesn't get much better for a hockey player than life as a member of the Maple Leafs. Even when you go on the road, you'll see Toronto jerseys in every store window, and you find Toronto fans everywhere. I had a great time in Toronto, but it was a crazy time. We had a pretty decent team, making the playoffs two of my three years. But when I was there, it was a strange time. Harold Ballard owned the team. Players were being traded inadvisably. Darryl Sittler and Ian Turnbull were traded when I was there. Both were trades that shouldn't have happened. Ballard would get rid of guys because he'd get mad at them. Sittler should never have been traded. He should have been a Leaf his whole career, but he and Ballard got into an argument over something. Same with Turnbull, Borje Salming, and Lanny McDonald. They all should have retired as Maple Leafs. All of them were household names, and Sittler, McDonald, and Salming are in the Hall of Fame. Good organizations make sure the faces of a team stay with the team and finish their careers there.

Ballard was a strange duck. We'd arrive at the rink and the door to the medical room would be closed. We'd show up a little early to have various injuries treated, but the door would be shut because Harold Ballard was inside getting his feet manicured, his toenails cut, and his corns taken care of by our trainers. A guy could be sitting outside with a separated shoulder, and he'd have to wait until Harold's feet were taken care of.

7

Losing a Step

fter three years with the Leafs, I signed as a free agent with Detroit. Toronto wanted to re-sign me, but would only give me a two-way contract – one salary for the NHL, and a much lower one for the American Hockey League. Detroit had watched me play, liked what they had seen, and offered me a two-year, one-way contract. With Toronto, that clause enabling them to save money by sending me down was right there in the contract, not a good omen.

A two-year, one-way deal looked pretty good to me, and Detroit had a lot of history. I loved the winged-wheel crest; it's a great jersey that is so perfect for sports, perfect for hockey, because of the way it incorporates the city and team. I enjoyed the idea of playing there, so I went to Detroit. We bought a beautiful house in the suburbs and had a second baby. We'd had our first son, Tyrell, in Toronto. We had Adrien in Detroit. My wife was busy. Life was good.

The Red Wings were rebuilding. They'd had a bad run behind a weak front office and had finished near the bottom of the NHL for several years. But they had a new owner, a new general manager, and had used their high draft picks to get some great young talent. The bright side of this situation, for me, was that I'd get more ice time, and as a veteran, I could be useful as a mentor for the younger players who were just starting out in the NHL.

Almost everyone on the Red Wings was new. We were just coming together, so we weren't exactly a contender. It was Steve Yzerman's rookie year. Stevie was going to be very good, but he was just getting started. We had veteran Brad Park, one of my favourite guys. Next to Bobby Orr, Brad had been the best defenceman in the NHL for a lot of years, in fact, he'd been the runner-up for the Norris Trophy six times; always losing it to Orr. He was at the end of his career by the time he joined Detroit, and he'd slowed down, but even then, as you watched him play, you could still see a lot of the things that made him great. Brad really knew how to move the puck.

Most players start dropping off, losing a step, in their early thirties. Chris Chelios, Nicklas Lidstrom, Jaromir Jagr, and others who play into their forties are freaks. A lot of it is avoiding bad injuries. But even if you've escaped a serious injury, as you hit your thirties your knees aren't working quite as well. Or maybe you've had a few smaller shoulder or hand injuries, or taken hits to the wrists that didn't seem that bad. Old injuries that seemed minor at the time come back to haunt you as you age, and figure heavily in how long you can play.

I was in Detroit parts of four seasons. I was up and down between them and the Adirondack Red Wings, Detroit's AHL farm team based in Glens Falls, New York. My first year, I played in Detroit most of the time. After that, I spent most of my time playing for Adirondack.

I've always been very honest about my career and my talent. I always knew that, for me, there was a chance of being sent down. And it had happened early on in my career, when I went to Springfield. But I was young then, and it had been a brief stay.

I'd been sent down again during my third year in Toronto. Management decided they wanted to go with all young guys on defence, so they sent me to play with the St. Catharines Saints in Ontario. I was there a couple of months, and it was difficult because by that time I'd been in the NHL seven years. When I returned to the Leafs, I played well, and a lot. The time in St. Catharines probably made me a better player. It's like I have said, when something happens that you think is terrible, wait a while before you judge it. Don't jump off any buildings, because sometimes it's really good for you.

While with Detroit, much as I hated to admit it, I was getting older. I was nearing thirty. I had always been one of those guys who had to work hard to make the team at the start of the season, and who had to battle to keep his job. But I had confidence. I knew I should be in the NHL, but I never had illusions about my talent level. I knew I was always a couple of bad games away from the AHL.

I was still a fighting defenceman. I wasn't just a fighter, I held my own as a player. But fighting was part of my role. Dropping the gloves and taking guys on never got old or difficult for me because I knew I had to do it. There's an old saying in hockey: "When a crusher becomes a rusher, he will soon be an usher." That simply means that when a tough guy forgets what his job is, he will soon be out of the game. I've seen that saying played out more than once, so I knew what I needed to do to stay in hockey. And I was willing to do it. I would have done anything to stay in hockey.

Being a pure fighter is hard, right from the start of your career. Guys who fight for a living, who have to keep dropping their gloves to protect their teammates, have a hard road. Their hands are always bruised, they get hurt taking punches, and they never know how much they're going to play. They might get only two shifts a night and have to fight during one of them. They've got to get out there and deliver hits every night. If they're tired or hurt, it doesn't matter. They're paid to play physically. And all the time they know there are five guys in the minors who are scrambling and clawing to take their job away. It's a very tough way to make a living. You've got to applaud the guys who do it night in and night out.

As I was getting older and slower, Detroit was getting better. They drafted Nick Lidstrom, they had Yzerman, Joey Kocur, and Bob Probert, and then they got Sergei Fedorov.

Fedorov was one of the first Russian stars to play in the U.S. The Soviet Union was allowing older guys to come over and end their careers here. But Fedorov actually had to defect. Detroit's coach, Nick Polano, was one of the guys who got him out. Nick says it was like a spy movie. Fedorov was playing a tournament in Italy. The Detroit officials attending the tournament got a message to him to meet them at a bar. Fedorov snuck out of the Russian hotel in the wee hours and met the Detroit guys. They put him in the trunk of the car and drove across the Swiss border. He was among the first great Russian players to come over.

Detroit was making good draft decisions, good trades, and it started to show. They made the playoffs the first two years I was there, missed a year or two in the late '80s, and have been in the playoffs ever since. In 2012, Detroit made the playoffs for the twenty-first straight year.

I got sent down again my first year in Detroit. It was in December, and it was my first really long stay in the minors. It was supposed to be just for two weeks, but it ended up being over a month. It's disheartening when you've been playing in the NHL for a while, enjoying that level of play and the spotlight that goes with it. And the money, of course. I'd been two years in Cincinnati, two years in Winnipeg, three years in Toronto, and one year in Detroit. I'd been playing pretty much full time in the NHL for a long time. To walk into that room and hear you're being sent down is one of life's very dark moments for a professional athlete. They always try to put a good spin on it: you're not playing much, we need to get you more ice time, you'll be back soon, all that crap, but it's a tough pill to swallow. Then you have to call your wife and tell her you're going down, and that changes her life. We had a young baby, so it changed his life, too. It's hard.

When I got into coaching, I really thought I'd be a better coach because of the stuff I had been through as a player. When those difficult situations came up, I really tried to think of the player. You still have to do the job – tell him he's traded, or sent down, whatever the bad news is – but it can certainly be done better than the times it happened to me.

Typically, they call you into the office and tell you to sit down. What the coach says depends on what kind of a guy he is. Some coaches say, "We're making changes with our minor-league system and we want you there." Others try to sugar-coat it. Some coaches blatantly lie to you and say it's temporary and that you'll be back up very soon.

When I had to do it as a coach, I was honest with the player. I treated him with respect. I tried to handle it like a man. I didn't lie to him or bullshit him. It's one of those conversations that, no matter what the coach says, the player is not going to be happy, so I would much rather the coach be honest. That way, when the guy leaves the room, he knows exactly where he stands.

Being sent down was the worst thing that happened to me as a player. Telling guys they were traded or sent down was the worst thing I had to do as a coach.

In Detroit, Nick Polano said, "We haven't been able to play you much. You're going to go down. We're only going to send you down for two weeks." I'd been around long enough to know that two weeks could mean forever. So I handled it like that. I was going down and I didn't know when I'd be back up.

To be honest, I didn't really think I was slowing down, losing any steps. And like I said, I was still playing my role, dropping the gloves when required. But some coaches like you and some coaches don't. For whatever reason, I never thought the coaching staff in Detroit gave me a chance. But that's neither here nor there. I was a professional and I was going to play hard wherever I went. The coaching staff make moves at their discretion. They're the coaches, they call the shots. That's how it works.

I had begun that year playing quite a bit, then less and less, and all of the sudden I was what they call a "healthy scratch." Part of it was my fault. I never went into Nick Polano's office and talked it out with him. Looking back, I should have gone in to see him and said, "Look, tell me why I'm not playing. Give me a chance to change your mind, and if I can't, then do what you will – trade me, send me down, whatever." As a coach, I wanted my players to come in, pound on my desk, and say they wanted to be the guy. But as a player, I didn't understand that.

As a kid, my parents had taught me to keep my mouth shut and assume the coach will make the right decisions. I was brought up to respect the voice of authority. If my dad or grandfather said something, that was the final word. I wish I'd had more of a tendency to challenge authority when I was playing. I should have walked in on Nick Polano, pounded his desk, and demanded he take another look at me. But I didn't.

The Adirondack Red Wings were in just their fifth season in the American Hockey League. (Before that, the Red Wings' farm team was in the Central Hockey League, in Kansas City.) I'd played in the American league for a month in the '70s, and had a few short trips down to St. Catharines the previous season, so I'd been to a lot of the AHL arenas. But this was a fairly new team with a new arena.

I had to get to Glens Falls, New York, the same night the coach gave me the news. I barely had enough time to rush home, pack, and go to the airport for a flight from Detroit to Albany. In Albany, I got in a cab and said I needed to go to Glens Falls. The driver said that was a long way. Turns out it was a fifty-mile cab ride. We started driving north, and pretty soon we were in a snowstorm, a heavy snowstorm. I'm from Saskatchewan, so I know my snowstorms, and this one was for real. After we had driven north more than forty minutes, I asked how much farther it was. The driver said it was "a ways." So we kept driving, and it was snowing like mad. There were snowbanks everywhere.

After another half-hour we finally arrived at this nice hotel, the Queensbury. It was two in the morning. There were piles and piles of snow everywhere. I was lugging my equipment and my luggage through the snow to the hotel room. I didn't know where I was. But it was beautiful. It looked like Bedford Falls, the town in *It's a Wonderful Life*. Remember the scene with Jimmy Stewart running down the street in the snowstorm with a couple of feet of snow on the ground? That's what Glens Falls looked like that night.

I grew up in winter. I enjoy the snow at the start of winter, when it's beautiful. But I had no idea where I was, stuck in some small northern town. I had just driven north on the interstate and never seen another car. I hadn't seen a rink, and the town looked very small. I was a very dejected hockey player at that moment in my life. I was in the middle of nowhere, buried in snow. I thought my life was over.

The next morning, I woke up and had to carry my equipment down to the arena, which was about a half-mile walk. Luckily, they'd done some shovelling. It was a beautiful arena, and things started looking up. But that was the toughest day I'd had in hockey.

My wife and family had stayed in Detroit. I ended up coming back to Detroit after six weeks, and I stayed up the rest of the year. But I didn't play much. I knew the next year I would probably be down in the minors the whole time. That turned out to be the case.

I had a great reception with Adirondack. I knew some of the guys. Their coach, Bill Dineen, was a great one. But I was now in the American Hockey League, and that's a demotion. That's what hangs over your head. You're going to a new team with a lot of people you don't know. It seemed grim. But there's this magic thing that happens. Once you get on the ice everything falls into place, returns to normal. Practice is practice. That seems to fix everything if you're a hockey player.

Adirondack was happy to have me. I was big and tough, and an NHL veteran, so it was great for them. I was going to play a lot. Getting acclimated and beginning to find my way around made for a confusing few days. But it turned out Glens Falls is a really nice spot, a beautiful, sleepy little town in upstate New York.

I didn't see my wife and family that whole time. There was no way to fly back for even a couple of days. In the AHL we played Wednesday, Friday, Saturday, and Sunday. And we travelled by bus. You don't fly in the AHL. In those days, the AHL was basically an east coast league, with teams from Baltimore, Maryland, up into the Maritime provinces, so we were bused everywhere we went.

Over the next couple of seasons, I played more and more for Adriondack. I still got called up to Detroit, but those calls became less frequent. Brad Park ended up coaching Detroit for a year. Brad liked me, so I was up in Detroit playing in ten or fifteen games my second year. But by then, Cindy and the boys had moved to Glens Falls. When I got called up my last year, we were separated again. This time I was in Detroit, and my family was in Glens Falls. That's how the game is.

I finished out that year with Adirondack and signed another one-year contract with Detroit, realizing I was going to finish my career in the AHL. But I was still making good money, and I was still playing the game I loved. Playing hockey was – and still is – the greatest job in the world.

You're in the American Hockey League, and you know that the end of your career is inevitable. That's when you start thinking seriously about your options. What am I going to do after I can't play anymore? How long do I want to continue to play in the American league? Am I happy doing this? Should I look at something else? I had two young kids. There's a lot of stuff that comes into play. My game plan those last years was to play as long as I could, then work on getting into coaching, and learn more about that job.

I would play in the AHL and hope to work with the kids Detroit was trying to develop. Schooling young players would help me learn more about coaching. I talked to my Adirondack coach, Bill Dineen, about my ambitions. Bill agreed to give me some coaching assignments. It turned into a nice plan. In the AHL there are always a bunch of young players, so Bill gave me a chance to work with them as a player/assistant coach, under his supervision and guidance. Dineen was a veteran coach, very well thought of, so it was a perfect scenario for me.

Being an assistant with Adirondack got me even more focused on the job, helped me make the transition from being a cog in the wheel to being the guy at the wheel.

8

From Player to Alchemist

My playing career ended with Adirondack in 1987. I had torn my knee up the previous year and had been in a cast for six months. It was a really bad injury. During a game, a guy hit my knee from the side and blew it out. It wasn't a dirty hit. I just happened to have my foot planted when he hit me on the side of the knee.

I played the next year. I still enjoyed it, but my knee hurt enough to make me wonder how much longer I could keep on. By 1987, I was a player and an assistant coach. I was working with the younger guys and helping them along. Detroit liked what I was doing. But I felt like it was time to move on. I decided I wanted to be a coach. That was a job I'd been thinking about for a long time. I figured if I were going to coach, I might as well jump into it with both feet. In 1988, I left Adirondack and started coaching.

As I've said, hockey is a small universe. It's easy, if you're in the game and you keep your eyes open, to know what's going on around the various leagues. I knew, for instance, that the Medicine Hat Tigers in the major junior Western Hockey League, needed a coach. I also knew that would be a good place to start my coaching career. Bill Dineen at Adirondack liked what I had done as player/coach. So he called Russ Farwell, the general manager in Medicine Hat, on my behalf. I went for an interview and I got the job.

It was a great situation. Medicine Hat had just won the Memorial Cup, the Stanley Cup of junior hockey. I'd be walking into a really good team. That was great. And I knew a lot of guys in the WHL, so it was like going home. It was an awesome chance for me.

There was a lot of stress for my family because we were moving again. We had been in Glens Falls long enough for it to feel like home. It was a great place to raise a family. Alberta, in western Canada, was a long way to move with two young kids. But it was a very exciting time, too. I was returning to the Western Hockey League, this time as a coach.

I'd always found the chemistry of a team fascinating – wondered why certain players worked hard for certain people, why certain coaches won all the time. I was eager to get into the details of building a team, figuring out what a team needs to win, what combinations of players were effective. I had always found those dynamics interesting. Having been assistant coach my last year, I had begun to focus on coaching more than ever. Now I was looking forward to being a head coach and living or dying with my own decisions.

One of the first things I found myself thinking about when I considered coaching was all the people I'd played for. You line up all your old coaches in your mind and recall that you liked playing for a certain guy, and you start trying to figure out why that was. You remember another guy who was terrible to play for, and again, why was that? You also think about what teams you played on, and why one team worked and another didn't. You think about teams you liked and dressing rooms you liked.

Now I was going to be that guy I'd spent all those years working for – and wanting to kill at times. It was time to put my money where my mouth was, because I was going to be making the decisions, handling things.

Coaching in general is a whole new world. As a player, you worry about one guy: yourself. When you're playing, your life is very structured because the coach tells you where to be, when to be there, where you're staying, when you're eating. That rigid structure is a part of playing that a lot of guys can't handle. Then, oddly enough, when they stop playing, they can't handle the *lack* of structure. They can't handle *not* being told what to do.

When you transition into coaching, you have to move from having the type of mentality that, as a player, allows you to respond to the controlling military structure, to being the guy who is telling the players where to be, how to dress, and what to eat. Even though I was a player/coach in Adirondack, I was still operating as an enlisted man. The very next year, I switched roles to commanding officer. One day I was a player, the guy following the rules. The next day, I was the coach, and I was getting the bus trips organized, booking the hotels, making up room lists, putting kids with the right billets. At the same time, I had a wife and two small kids. It was almost like having two families.

There's team practice every day, and you're also making sure your players are getting to school and keeping their marks up. You're talking to their teachers and tutors to forestall any problems. It's a mind- and eye-opening experience when you get into coaching. As a player, you had no idea how much your life was controlled by your coach, or how many different things that coach was responsible for. I learned all that quickly.

As coach, you're also the disciplinarian. That's another thing: discipline. I played for some real hard-ass coaches that I liked, and I played for some very fair coaches that I liked. I had to figure out where I was going to land in that range. You can't coach a bunch of players without having discipline. But you can't be such a dick that it turns people off and makes them not want to play for you. I was enthusiastic about taking on those problems and figuring out how to solve them.

I had played a long time, and had been lucky to share the ice with some really great players. I'd learned a lot about the game and had a head full of ideas I wanted to try. I was very excited about coaching. I know how important chemistry is. A team's chemistry is basically created by the general manager and the coach. Together, those guys put the team together. To begin with, there has to be good chemistry between the two of them. The GM can't be drafting a lot of skill players when the coach wants toughness, or vice versa. Those two have to have a meeting of the minds, and agree to collaborate on how to best attain the common goal: winning.

It's interesting how a team is built. If it's a good team, all the pieces are there – all the various talents – and they fit. If it's not such a good team, you might have all the pieces, but for whatever reason, they don't work together. You might have a dressing room full of talented guys, but they might all hate each other. Hockey is such a tough sport, and the season is so long, that if you don't enjoy the guys you are with – if you don't love the dressing room – you can't wait for the season to be over.

The team that will win the Stanley Cup is the team that can't wait for the next season to start, that can't wait to get back together again. If you're on a bad team, the summer goes by fast because you aren't looking forward to seeing each other again. Winning teams have a special bond. There are a lot of talented teams, like the 2011 Red Sox in baseball, who don't win. Man for man, the Washington Capitals of 2010 and 2011 were hard to beat on paper. But the chemistry wasn't there.

There's a saying in sports: "Will beats skill." On paper, teams like the Capitals and the San Jose Sharks should be winning. Both lineups are full of talent, every bit as good as Detroit, Boston, or Vancouver. But they don't come close. They don't have that intangible something, that fear of losing. They don't get better as the games get tougher.

An individual example is Evgeni Malkin in Pittsburgh. At the close of the 2011–12 regular season, Sidney Crosby had been out most of two years with concussion issues. Malkin stepped up. He accumulated more points without Crosby than he had with him in the lineup. He raised his level of play. That's what great players do, and that's what winning teams do. Teams like the Washington Capitals, with all their talent, don't do that.

When they face a problem, they shrink. When great teams face a problem, they get bigger.

The players you see yapping in the press will usually be from disjointed teams, teams without chemistry. You don't see the New England Patriots' players complaining, or players from Green Bay mouthing off. Players from the good, stable teams, like the Boston Bruins, the Red Wings, or the Vancouver Canucks, don't complain. The good teams love being together. They are cohesive units who like each other, who love playing together, who love their dressing rooms, and who have figured out how to win.

In Medicine Hat, I wanted to build a team of the sort I didn't like to play against. I wanted a team that was very fast, because I felt speed was the future of the game. I wanted a team that was brave, because I feel courage is an essential part of hockey. I wanted a team that was physical, to intimidate other teams we played against. And I wanted a really talented team, because those were the guys who scared me as a player. I was never scared of big, tough guys. I was always scared of the fast, talented guys because they caused a lot of problems. Those were the guys who could make you look stupid. The speed guys were the ones who kept me up at night.

A lot of those elements existed in Medicine Hat. I walked into a team, that had just won the Memorial Cup, the junior championship of Canada. The Tigers were a very good team, and they had a lot of the things that I wanted. But it took a long time to get to these kids. Their coach had advanced to the NHL – that's why there was a coaching opening at Medicine

This is the Foam Lake Bantam team. Bernie Federko is wearing the "C" and that's me beside him. I was fourteen at the time. I had been loaned to Foam Lake to play in the provincials, which we won that year.

The Weyburn Redwings in the 1973–74 season. I'm in the middle of the back row, the tallest guy there.

I made the WCHL all-star team my last year of junior. A lot of these guys went on to play in the NHL. That's me in the middle row, beside the checkered blazer.

Reggie Kerr was my defence partner on the Kamloops Chiefs my first year in the WCHL (1975). We roomed together the two years I was there.

The Montreal Canadiens drafted me in the second round and sent this contract, signed by the great Scotty Bowman.

CLUB DE HOCKEY CANADIEN, INC.

2313 St. Catherine Street West   Tel.: 932-6131   Montreal 108, P.Q.

Via Registered Mail
Return Receipt Requested

It is a pleasure to invite you to the 1976 training camp which will commence on Wednesday, September 15th at the Forum in Montreal.

An extensive physical examination will be given by the medical department at 9.00 a.m. on September 15th at the Forum.

For out of town players rooms have been reserved at the BERKELEY HOTEL, 1188 Sherbrooke Street West, Montreal, telephone (514) 849-7351.

Please arrange your own travel and upon arrival in Montreal present receipts and you will be reimbursed. If you plan to travel to camp by automobile, please obtain prior clearance from us here. Also, if you have your skates at home, kindly bring them with you.

Our opening pre-season game will be on Saturday, September 18th so pre-training camp activity by you is advised.

Trusting you and your family are enjoying a happy Summer and looking forward to seeing you at training camp, I am,

Very truly yours,

Scott Bowman

Encl.
SB:D:sl

Scott Bowman,
Coach.

P.S. - PLEASE COMPLETE THE ATTACHED QUESTIONNAIRE AND RETURN IT TO US IMMEDIATELY IN THE ENVELOPE PROVIDED.

This is my draft party at the Kelvington Golf Club. My dad's on the far left, my mom's over my shoulder, and my grandparents are beside her.

When I was twenty, the Stingers flew me and Greg Carroll down to Cincinnati to show us around the city. This is us at a Reds game.

I played twenty-three games with the Springfield Indians at the start of the 1976–77 season before I got called up to the WHA for good.

The Cincinnati Stingers' lineup from my first season in the pros.

The Honeybees were the Cincinnati Stingers' cheerleading squad. That's my future wife, Cindy, in the middle row, second from the right.

Scotty Campbell and I had some good fights back in the WHA days. We ended up playing together in Winnipeg after the leagues merged.

When the WHA and NHL merged, my rights reverted back to the Canadiens, the NHL team that drafted me. I got traded to the Jets before I ever played a game with the Habs.

Detroit signed me in the 1983–84 season, but I would spend most of my time with the organization playing for their farm team in Adirondack.

The Kelvington Golf Club put up pictures of all the local NHLers. That's me and Wendel Clark posing in front of our billboards.

Adirondack won the Calder Cup my second season there. That's me behind the bench in 1992.

The night the Kings beat the Leafs to win the Campbell Conference trophy in 1993. That's Kings' owner Bruce McNall in the foreground on the left, and my assistant coach, Cap Raeder, just right of me.

We had a lot of celebrities visit during the 1993 run in L.A., but none was bigger than former president Ronald Reagan. He and Nancy didn't miss a game.

That's me, the Geico caveman, and Steve Levy in front of the Green Monster at Boston's Fenway Park for the 2010 Winter Classic.

Left to right, that's Hugo Belanger, me, the Hansons, Frank Littlejohn, and Bobby Hull at the Adam Oates Celebrity Golf Classic.

Hat. He'd been with them a number of years and had taken them to the top of the heap. That was something of a disadvantage for me. They hated seeing their coach move on. They were probably happy for him, but sad, and probably feeling a little rejected for being left behind.

They weren't exactly ready to embrace his replacement. I was like their mother's new boyfriend, an object of resentment – a jerk until proven otherwise. Not only was I the new coach, but I had no coaching experience. They didn't know me from Adam, and I didn't know them. There was going to be a lot of testing going on both ways.

Our season started in October, and it took until December before they bought into my act. I had a lot to learn. I had to learn it's not what you say, it's what they hear. And I had to learn about discipline.

When you're coaching junior hockey, you're coaching young kids. I went from dealing with men in the NHL and the AHL to coaching kids between sixteen and nineteen years old. As the coach, you're not only establishing the rules, you are enforcing them. Making the rules is the easy part. Enforcing them is the hard part. You have to decide what rules you really believe in – what rules make sense and are productive – and what kind of team you want to produce.

I've practised a million times in my life, but as a coach you're running practices every day, developing drills, and that's just the beginning. In those days, there was only one coach. I didn't have an assistant. It was quite a wake-up call to find out all that was involved with being a coach. Several things caught me by surprise.

One day, I was mad at the guys. Practice had been sloppy. I was in my office, moping about the situation, when this guy walked in who had volunteered to help me with the job, running some practices and doing odd jobs around the rink. He was a local schoolteacher, a former player who loved the sport. We were sitting in my office, having a coffee. I was venting about the team. When I finished, there was a pause, and then he said, "Barry, let me tell you something. You've got twenty kids here. They know exactly what they want to be. They are motivated enough to have left home. They all want to play in the NHL more than anything in the world. You should come over to my school sometime. I've got four hundred kids the same age as the kids on your team. They have no idea what they want to do. Most of them don't want to be anything. Most of them don't want to be in school. They have no work ethic. Most of them are very difficult kids. Some are downright bad. In my eyes, you're the luckiest guy in the world to be working with twenty of the most motivated kids in this whole town."

That was one of the most important things anyone has ever said to me. That teacher was so right. I was lucky to have such a bunch of great, highly motivated kids. As a coach I could – and did – get mad at these guys, but I could never forget they were unusual kids. They had all made big sacrifices to take a shot at playing in the NHL, and it was my job to get them there. Reaching that understanding made me a better coach, no doubt about it.

One of my surprises as a junior hockey coach was the amount of time I had to spend working with those kids as guidance counsellor, father figure, therapist, and recruiter. A junior coach wears all those hats. It begins with going into people's homes and meeting with kids that are fifteen years old. You've got to talk the parents into giving you their kids. It's a formidable task. That's the recruiting part, although it's not heavy recruiting because the vast majority of talented Canadian players want to enter junior hockey. We lost a couple of kids to the American colleges, but not many. And in Medicine Hat, we had an attractive team, having just won the Memorial Cup the year before. We were a solid franchise, but you still had to go in person to seal the deal with these young kids and their parents.

Very few parents were difficult. They weren't like what you hear about overly aggressive Little League parents in the U.S. who drive coaches crazy. Most of them didn't understand the complexities of the system their sons were joining, from recruitment to signing. They only had the vaguest idea of how the business worked. All they knew was they were going to lose their boy. Mothers especially suffer that. So you had to go in and convince both parents that you were going to be good to their boy, watch over him, and take care of him, the way Dwight MacMillan had done for me when I went to Weyburn.

That's why, when any sexual-abuse controversy happens, like the business at Penn State in 2011, it cuts me to the quick, because I know how much power coaches have over kids. It really sickens me to hear about people who have taken advantage of that situation, taken advantage of that power the coach has over fifteen- through eighteen-year-old kids. It's just a horrible thing. It gives everybody a black eye.

We had one of those scandals during the time I was coaching at Medicine Hat. It involved the junior team in Swift Current, Saskatchewan – the Broncos. It didn't come out until later, but that was when it was going on. I was at Medicine Hat. Graham James was the coach at Swift Current. A boy named Sheldon Kennedy came forward and blew the whistle on his coach. It took a long time for that case to develop, but James was eventually convicted.

Kennedy had to do it alone because hockey players are a very macho group. They would be the last group to come forward on an issue like that. Kennedy was very frustrated that no one else raised his hand, because he knew more players had been abused.

Having been sexually abused is a very hard thing to talk about, so it wasn't surprising to anybody in hockey that more people didn't come forward. Theo Fleury, a top scorer in junior hockey who went on to have a great NHL career with five different teams, just came forward in the last few years. His autobiography, *Playing with Fire*, published in 2009, addressed his abuse at the hands of Graham James and helped re-convict James.

I know Sheldon Kennedy wanted Theo to come forward when the abuse was going on, but Theo wasn't ready. I don't judge Theo, because until you are in his place, you can't criticize. Hopefully, no one else will ever be in that place. It has to be very traumatic. If you blow the whistle, it's like you have to live through it twice: once when it happens, and again when you announce it. That was one of the problems. No one else would come forward and back Sheldon up.

Kennedy was applauded for taking what was a very brave stand. Many people think his willingness to expose his coach was a wake-up call, a turning point in the realm of harassment and sexual abuse in sports.

Fortunately, that sort of scandal was very rare. I played junior hockey, I coached junior hockey, and that was the only incident I saw in my ten years in junior hockey. It was a terrible, isolated situation.

Thankfully, my problems in Medicine Hat were more like those of a surrogate parent. One thing you're dealing with when you're coaching kids at that age is their parents divorcing. It's more prevalent now than when I was coaching in '88, but it was a factor. During one season, we had a player's mother die of cancer. The kids are very vulnerable at that age. They have all sorts of growing pains. Being away from home, usually for the first time, doesn't help.

If a kid goes into a funk in junior hockey, it could be because a girlfriend is breaking up with him. He could be having trouble at school. It can be so many things, and they all fall into the coach's lap. A coach has to know his players well enough to know how to best help them through those life traumas.

They were great kids in Medicine Hat, so motivated, so happy to be playing a game they loved. I wasn't making much money, but coaching junior was one of the favourite things I had done in hockey.

There was a lot to learn. I had a bunch of ideas I was eager to try. I was intrigued by fancy breakouts I'd seen coming from European players. In a breakout, the defenceman stands behind his own net with the puck and stops for a moment. His team cruises into attack mode while the other team sends in fore-checkers and gets ready for them to come out. You use a breakout playing five-on-five once in a while, and on the power play quite a bit.

I had all these grand ideas that involved everybody swinging in different directions, looking like ballet on the ice, as a way to get the breakout started. I had all these plays drawn up – a playbook, a drill book. I was going to reinvent the game of hockey.

Before we started playing the Europeans, North American hockey was linear. The right winger stayed on the right, the left winger stayed on the left, the centre went wherever he wanted, and the defencemen stayed left and right and didn't go into the other team's end very often. The guys overseas changed all that.

Canada first played the Russians in 1972. It was called the Summit Series, eight games – four in Canada, four in the Soviet Union – between the best professional players from both countries. It might have been the greatest hockey series ever played. The Soviets were supposed to be outmatched by Canada's powerful roster; in fact, after the four games in Canada and one in Moscow, the Soviet Union had taken three games, Canada had won just one, and one had ended in a tie. Canada had to win the last three games, all to be played in Moscow, to take the series, and they did. They did it without Bobby Orr, who was hurt, and Bobby Hull, who was with the WHA (and so had not been allowed to join the team). It was huge. I don't think there was a soul in Canada who wasn't watching those games on television. A Toronto Maple Leafs left winger named Paul Henderson scored the winning goal in all three games to make him one of Canada's most famous athletes to this day.

We were all shocked by the Russians' style of hockey, with the swinging breakouts, guys crossing in front of the puck handler or coming up behind him so he could drop the puck to them. A guy might be going left, and then suddenly he would drop the puck to a buddy streaking the other way behind him. Or maybe a guy would just change lanes, use some other creative way to bring the puck up ice.

It was quite a change to see every player basically free of his zone, playing each other's positions, mixing it up, being a creative unit of five skaters. It was totally improvisational hockey. It stunned Canadians, changed the way we envisioned the game. Today's game is a hybrid between European and North American hockey.

When I was a player, I found that European open style very hard to defend against. So as a coach, I wanted to use that style, teach the guys how to do it. I wanted my team to play using a much more open style. I wanted to stress creativity and imagination. I never wanted the players to be leery of trying things. I always told them they'd never get in trouble with me for doing that. It was especially important that talented guys could feel free to try things. I'd always accept mistakes made out of aggression. I never condoned complacency, always favoured creativity. As long as you were working your butt off, I'd accept just about anything you did – unless it was something stupid like trying to beat somebody in front of your own net.

But I soon discovered that a lot of the things I wanted to do had to be put on the shelf because the kids weren't good enough to do them. I was used to dealing with men who played hockey for a living, and I'd been playing with some of the best. In the AHL, you've got some of the best rookies from the NHL teams, guys who are there just long enough to fine-tune great talent. And you've got some accomplished veterans. You can try all kinds of new wrinkles with those guys. But when you get back to junior hockey, you're working with sixteen-year-old kids who are just developing. They aren't ready for fancy anything. That was one of my learning experiences. I had to dial down my skill-level expectations, put my playbooks on the shelf.

My idea of discipline also had to be modified. In the AHL, you've got beer on the buses, beer in the dressing room. Again, you're dealing with men. With sixteen-year-old kids, you have different issues. And you're now the authority figure, so you've got to do things right with the kids, handle them properly. You're on call all the time. With professionals, you don't start worrying about them until they get to the rink. When you're coaching these kids, you're talking to their teachers and their parents 24/7.

I hadn't been in Medicine Hat long when one of my veteran players called and said he had a problem and needed to talk. I told him to come on over. I was sitting there in my office and thinking, "This is great. I'm going to do some coaching here. I'm going to do some mentoring. Here's a chance for me to change a young man's life. I can really have a positive effect on this young man's life."

The kid comes in – he's nineteen years old – and he sits down across from me. I'm ready to talk about some school issues, or maybe he was having some trouble at home with his parents – really deep stuff. I'm poised and prepared.

He says, "Barry, I need to talk with you about my billet. I'm having problems with my billet." I think, "Okay, it's got to be something about nutrition. Maybe he's not getting enough food, or the wrong types of food." I'm thinking about that when he says, "Barry, where I live, the husband is a long-haul trucker. Whenever he goes away on a four- or five-day trip, the woman comes down to my room and I have to make love to her all night long. I'm not getting any sleep and it's really affecting how I feel, how I'm playing."

That was the first problem I had to handle as a coach in junior hockey.

We moved the kid out and dropped that couple from the billet lists. I'm sure that resulted in a lot of disappointed young men in junior hockey.

Taking care of these kids went all the way to managing their immigration cards. When the cards came in, I had to keep them. If I handed them out, they would have been lost. Professionals, adult hockey players, often lost their cards, so I was sure that a bunch of juniors would. When we got to the border on road trips, I'd have to take all their papers in and process them.

There were no limits to a junior coach's off-ice duties. Anything that could happen with a group of headstrong, immature athletes, would happen. You just had to be ready all the time.

At one point, the Tigers had ten road games over a two-week period, a tough bit of scheduling. The captain came to me and said the boys would like to have a little get-together at one of the village places. I said, "Okay, but here are the rules: make sure everybody is there, that no one drives after he's had a few beers, and that nobody gets crazy. That means nobody drinks too much." But I gave them the go-ahead because I had great kids and I trusted them.

I got a call at four o'clock in the morning from my captain, saying there was a problem with a certain player. A lot of guys on the team didn't really like this guy, and it's true, he was a bit of a jerk, but the captain told me four of our guys were ready to kill this guy. So at four in the morning I drive over, and sure enough, there's this guy, drunk in front of someone's house, reeling around, surrounded by a bunch of teammates who want to beat the crap out of him. He was taunting his mates, talking trash, saying things like they would never play in the NHL. This kid was a high draft pick, so he was cocky. That was a big status symbol in junior hockey – how high you had been drafted. They threw that at each other a lot, especially when taunting on the ice. At that age, they all think they will be NHL stars. They've been stars their whole lives. They haven't faced adversity yet. They haven't been humbled.

Of course, when you get liquor involved, everything gets accelerated. I had to get into it, settle that kid down, settle the other four guys down, then drive them all home.

My Medicine Hat Tigers were playing below their potential until we approached Christmas. Then there was an interesting development. Around Christmas, there's a tournament called the World Junior Championship. All the best hockey countries – Canada, the U.S., Russia, Latvia, Finland, Denmark, the Czech Republic, Sweden, Switzerland, Slovakia – enter teams. It's a huge annual tournament.

We had five kids from the Tigers selected for the Canadian team. During the Christmas season we had five games on the schedule that we'd have to play without those five kids. The first three games were on the road. There I was, with a team

that was playing .500 hockey, and I'd just lost my five best players to the World Junior team. The pressure was on. People on
the street were saying that if the Tigers weren't great *with* those
five exceptional players, how would they make out without
them? They expected us to lose all five games.

What happened was completely the opposite: we pulled it
together and won all five games. That turned the whole year
around. That experience made me a much better coach. I got
closer to the players during that time. When those five players
came back, we added them back into the team and we went on
to have a great season. We had a great playoff and won the
Memorial Cup again. It was only the fourth time since the
competition started, in 1919, that a team had won back-to-back
Memorial Cups.

Having to take on those five games shorthanded was the
best possible learning experience for me. I had to learn how to
coach my team, and the players had to learn how to play for
me. I had to really get to know each player, to learn which
player could do what, to learn how to handle each one. It took
me several months to figure all that out, but the compression
factor of those five games made it a do-or-die situation.

The turning point came on the road, during the first of
those five games, one night in Brandon, Manitoba. The guys
had a terrible first period. I blew into the dressing room. I was
mad. I had to figure out a way to motivate these guys. I did that
scene from the movie *Bull Durham*, where the guy throws the
bats at his players, throws the garbage can at them, calls them
"lollygaggers." I didn't use the word "lollygaggers," but freaking
out like that is Coaching 101. It scares the players.

I went a little crazy in the dressing room, throwing the benches around, knocking the Gatorade over, yelling at them, and really challenging them. That was the first time I'd gone off like that, and darned if they weren't a different team in the second period. We ended up winning that game, and all five in a row.

The guys always laughed at that when we looked back. They'd say, "Jeez, Barry, remember when you did that in Brandon? We thought you were going to kill us!"

As their coach, I wasn't really mad at them. I was just trying to change their state of mind. Well, in fact, I *was* mad at them, because they were not putting out enough effort – maybe not any effort. But the idea is to change their heads with some shock therapy. You can't do that too often, and you certainly can't do it every game. But every once in a while it can get their attention. It worked because, number one, they are kids. Kids are a lot easier to scare than adults. Number two, I'm a pretty big guy. That's something you can use as a coach – your physical size. Number three, I've got a big, loud voice. That works to my advantage. Number four, I'd had it done to me, so I knew it worked. There's a lot of history involved. When you start coaching, you remember what your old coaches did in certain situations. You take what works and try not to use what didn't work, and come up with inventions of your own. That's how you develop your coaching identity.

At the time, the kids hadn't bought into me or my system. They hadn't come to my way of thinking, hadn't started believing in the way I wanted the team to play. And I hadn't found the right buttons to push to make that happen. I hadn't learned who could do what, how much various players could take, who needed a kick in the butt, who needed a pat on the back. I was still learning. I'd just met these guys in September. I'd had them for two months. Both the team and I were learning on the job.

That dressing room scene in Brandon was a pivotal moment. I knew that if you get on a road trip and lose the first game, it can be like a snowball, resulting in a string of losses. But it can go either way. Because we won that game, our snowball was positive, and we won the first three of those games on the road. By the time we got home for the last two games, the fans were cranked and we were on a roll. Putting it all together was a huge challenge that the players and I were able to tackle together, and as a result, it put us over the top. The last three or four months of that season, we were the best team in junior hockey.

9

Coaching Attitude

I only spent one year in Medicine Hat. Russ Farwell, the Tigers' GM, the man who hired me, was going to Seattle, another city in the Western Hockey League. Russ was a good guy, a great GM. He would end up as the Philadelphia Flyers' general manager for five years – he's the guy who orchestrated the trade that brought Eric Lindros to Philly. He's back in Seattle right now as part-owner of the junior team.

Back when we were in Medicine Hat together, the Seattle owner had offered Russ a nice deal to turn the franchise around. The Thunderbirds had been a terrible team, the worst team in the league, but the owner had great plans for them. He wanted them to be a successful franchise, and he thought Russ could put it together for him.

Russ asked me to come with him to Seattle and be his coach. That was a tough moment, because Medicine Hat had just won those back-to-back Memorial Cups. After thinking about it, I told Russ I was going to have a talk with George Mazur,

Medicine Hat's owner, and tell him that I wanted both jobs — coach and GM — because I would love to take a run at winning a third-straight Memorial Cup for the franchise. That had never been done before. I thought we were going to be a pretty good team, and we had a definite shot at winning it again. Russ understood.

I went to George Mazur and told him I thought I could handle both jobs. I told him his team had a chance to win three straight Memorial Cups. George was very open to the idea. He thought it over and gave it the green light. The only problem was, he didn't want to pay me to do both jobs. Once I realized that, I decided I should go to Seattle. But I always regretted leaving Medicine Hat and not having the chance to win a third-straight Memorial Cup.

I enjoyed working with Russ. I learned a lot from him. Going to coach in Seattle turned out to be a very smart move.

When you coach junior hockey, the kids almost become your children. You have a great impact on their lives. I'm still friends with a lot of the kids I coached. I was in Pittsburgh in 2011 to watch the Penguins play the New York Islanders. A guy named Dean Chynoweth was one of the assistant coaches with the Islanders. Dean had been my captain at Medicine Hat. I went to see him, and it was just like old times.

In Seattle, after the season, the kids who were in school stayed in the city to finish the semester. As coach, I was still keeping an eye on them, making sure they were tending to business. One day, I got a call from the school, telling me one of my kids was missing classes, not showing up. It happened that this boy was

one of my favourite players. He was sixteen years old at the time.
He ended up playing the in the NHL and winning a Stanley Cup.
He was just a great, great kid. But the rule was, if you were staying in town after season, you had to go to school. Staying around
to sleep in or to avoid going home wasn't acceptable.

I went over to where this boy was billeting and told him to
pack up his clothes. Then I drove him to Vancouver, a two-hour
trip. On our way to Vancouver, I asked him what was going on.
He said he had a girlfriend he'd been spending a lot of time with.
I reminded him of the deal: if you stay in Seattle, you finish
school. He said he knew that. I told him he'd broken a promise
to me. I told him I was going to put him on a plane, and that he
was going home to finish school in Prince George. We had a
good talk. When I let him off at the airport, he was clear about
the situation.

Now he's a coach, and he's married with three kids. When
we meet, we joke about that day in Seattle. The interesting thing
is that he ended up marrying the same girl he had been missing
school to see. So his story had a happy ending.

I didn't have too many issues with parents when I coached
in junior hockey. I think the parents were different then – not
so aggressive. What you did have were agents, and lots of them.
Today, the agents, not the teams, own the kids. Players sign
with agents when they are as young as fourteen years old. And
when a kid is a high draft pick, the agents will be circling.
There's a lot of money in it for them, between 3 per cent and
9 per cent of what a player gets. So they want to make sure
that everything is going their player's way. Truth is, the agents
are a pain in the ass.

Coaches have their hands full with agents. At the start of the year, I always told my players that if they had a problem with me, they should come into my office and we'd solve it face to face. That's how men handle problems. I told them I did not want to see their agent. If their mom or dad wanted to call me, that would be fine. I'd be happy to talk with them. But problems would be taken care of between players and me. I guaranteed them if I had a problem with any of them, I was definitely not going to be calling their agent. I told them I would call them in, talk with them face to face, and that system would work both ways.

Nowadays, the players themselves are much more vocal. All parents seem to think their sons are going to be the next players to make ten million dollars a year. And the kids are talking big, and they all have agents, so now you've got a corps of agents trying to get info to you, selling you their clients. Because of all that, coaching junior hockey is even more complicated than it was.

It changed when the money got a lot bigger, probably around the year 2000. When I was coaching, all the kids had agents, but they weren't as aggressive as they are now. If you talk to a junior hockey coach today, he'll tell you about the constant pressure from parents and agents who are calling them if you bench their kid, or if you aren't giving the kid enough ice time. Everyone is very aggressive. It's the money. Everybody involved with the kid wants more influence. They all have a piece of the pie, and they all want their piece to be worth more.

Money means that you start promising these kids the world. Agents go into their homes and tell the kids they are going to be first-round picks. An agent tells a kid he's going to give him the world to get him to sign with them. It doesn't matter if the kid has no chance of being a first-round pick. I've seen a lot of slimy stuff over the years between agents and players.

I always question an agent having three or four players on the same team. Since everything is about money, what's to stop an agent from using his players as negotiating pieces, one against the other? He could say, "Sign this guy for what I want, and I'll give you this other guy for less." When an agent has two defencemen, or two forwards on the same team, that always looks like a conflict of interest to me.

That does happen, but not so much anymore. When I was playing, agents didn't have to be certified. It was like the Wild West out there. I could have been a player one day, an agent the next. Now, with the players' association in place, agents have to be certified. Contracts are examined by the players' association, so things have tightened up.

The difference between Medicine Hat and Seattle was experience. When I walked into the Medicine Hat dressing room, no one knew much about me as a player, and I'd never coached. But I walked into Seattle as the guy who had just won a second-straight Memorial Cup. Talk about instant credibility. Once you've won, you've proved to everyone you *can* coach, and you get a lot better reception.

I was only with the Thunderbirds for one year. Russ and I took over a terrible franchise. We had to change the whole culture of the team and the way the players approached the game. We had to reshuffle the lineup, get some new players, and change the way the veterans were playing. It was maybe the best coaching job I've ever done. We got things turned around by January, won our last seven games of the year, and just missed the playoffs. We actually tied for the last playoff spot, but lost out through the tie-breaker system the league used. By the end of the year, we were awesome. We had great young kids, our veterans were playing well, and I was really happy with how we had turned Seattle into a very good franchise in just one season.

Seattle was a tough assignment because losing had become a habit. As a coach, you are not only changing how the kids play, you're changing *why* they play, and how they think about playing. It was a long, difficult season, but it was very rewarding as a coach.

You can definitely coach attitude. There are many times when a coach has to change the culture of the dressing room. If you walk into a team that's used to losing, you've walked into a very precarious situation. You must find a way to reverse that trend. The coach's job is to make losing unacceptable. You have to make losing hard. You have to make losing hurt. A team that gets too comfortable with losing is a team that's not going to win anything.

Maybe you inherit a team that has been run like a country club, that has no discipline, that doesn't practise well. You have to change that into a culture of hard work. You have to let the team know that practices are expected to be crisp, strong, and tough on a daily basis. Or maybe you have a team that is scared to play. Maybe they have been brow-beaten and they have no confidence left. Then it's the coach's job to find a way to instill confidence, to build those players up.

Every time a coach walks into a dressing room for the first time, he'll see things that have to be changed. If you're the new coach, most of the time that means your predecessor wasn't doing a good job. Medicine Hat was an exception. Their coach went to the NHL because of his success, and that created a whole different set of problems. But most of the time, you have to change things. A big part of coaching is being able to identify what needs to be changed.

When I walked into Seattle, I found a team that had lost consistently for years. The players were good kids, but they accepted losing too easily. My job was to change that whole mindset. They had to learn to hate losing.

After a game, win or lose, the Seattle players were used to getting on the bus, listening to music, and falling asleep. One of the things I did was make them stay awake after a loss. I kept the lights on in the bus, and went so far as to sit at the back to make sure none of the players fell asleep. I'd stir them up. I told them, "I can't sleep after a loss, so I'll be damned if you're going to." That was one way I made losing miserable for them.

I made practices the day after a loss exhausting. They began to understand that losing meant repercussions, it had consequences. Before I got there, a loss was just another day at the rink. Sure, a win felt better than a loss, but in their minds there was no big difference between the two. I decided to create a significant difference in atmosphere after a loss. Making that happen basically took the whole season, but by the end of the season, as I said, we had won our last seven games. We were as good a team as there was in the Western Hockey League. By then, the kids had come around. No longer did they accept losing. That was the culture that I changed.

Players are smart. If, after every loss, the coach is making your life hell, and after the odd win life is great, it won't take them long to put two and two together and say, "Hey, the more we win, the better life is going to be." One thing that often happens in junior hockey is that, after a bad game, the coach will make the guys go out and skate. You can't do that in the NHL, but you find other ways to deliver the message. In the NHL, you can call practices at different times, make them come out earlier in the morning. And you make practices physical. You tell them, "If you guys can give this to me in the game, you don't have to do it in practice, but I'm either going to get it in the game or I'm going to get it in practice." The point is, you can never, ever let losing become acceptable in the dressing room. If you do that, you're done.

I never had a problem being challenged by a player because of how I was running the team. I told my players that if I never embarrassed them in front of the team, they should never embarrass me in front of the team. If they had a problem with me, I told them to come in and see me in my office and we would handle it there. If a player came into my office to talk about hockey, that meant he was thinking about hockey. That's a good thing. I just had to have faith in my ability to convince the team that what I was doing was right. The players knew I really did have an open-door policy. A guy would come in to complain, ask me why we were practising so hard, why were we practising at eight in the morning instead of eleven in the morning. I had to have faith that I could convince him why I was doing it.

A coach's attitude directly influences the team. A coach has to be consistently upbeat and positive. A team has a lot of ups and downs. A team is not going to win every game. So a coach has to know when to be positive and when to be negative. He has to know when to be a taskmaster, and when to ease up. But his attitude always directly influences the team.

If the players think the coach doesn't know what he's doing or they think he's doesn't know where he's going, why would they follow him? So the coach has to exude confidence in the dressing room. I agree with people who say that the coach sets the tone for a team. You hear it all the time: the team plays like the coach. If the coach is either a real hard-ass, or unsure of himself, or distracted, that's how the team will play.

10

The Whole Cake

After that season with the Seattle Thunderbirds, the Detroit Red Wings approached me about coming back into their organization and coaching my old AHL team in Glens Falls, the Adirondack Red Wings. Just as the American Hockey League is a stepping stone for players headed to or from the NHL, it's also a proving ground for young coaches. The vast majority of coaches in the NHL polished their skills in the AHL. So it was a natural progression for me.

Detroit had been watching what I had done in Medicine Hat and Seattle. I knew all the guys in the Detroit organization. Kenny Holland, whom I had played with in Adirondack, was now the head scout. Jimmy Devellano, who signed me to play in Detroit years earlier, was now signing me as a coach. We had the same owner, Mike Ilitch, arguably the best owner in hockey. He's owned the Detroit Red Wings for thirty years. And we had many of the same players – Steve Yzerman, Gerard Gallant, Bob Probert. And Bill Dineen, my old coach, was the GM at

Adirondack. It was a seamless transition. I'd only been away two years.

The hockey world is very small, and I've been in it since 1972. A lot of guys I played junior with are still in the game. That means we have been together for *forty years*. If I don't know somebody, the guy next to me will know him. Combine that with all the guys you've met in your career, and there's a tight network. Maybe you worked with somebody at a hockey school, or you met somebody at a party or a banquet in the summer, or at a golf tournament. Everybody seems to know everybody in our sport. And hockey people are very loyal to each other. We are very protective of our sport. We all think our sport is the greatest. We all think our athletes are the best. And we all help each other out.

I had some other opportunities. The Toronto Maple Leafs had approached me about being an assistant coach. But I wanted to be a head coach. I thought I was ready. So when Jimmy Devellano called me after the season and said he wanted me to coach Adirondack, it sounded great. I loved the Adirondack team, I had loved playing there, and I loved the Detroit organization. It was a no-brainer for me to decide we were going back to Glens Falls.

It was like going home. The whole family was excited about returning. It's a great place to live. I have a lot of friends there. We still own a house there today. When I accepted that job to go back to Glens Falls, it was one of the best moments of my life.

We had loved our time in Seattle. When you're coaching junior, it's difficult to leave a bunch of kids that have become your second family. Leaving both Medicine Hat and Seattle was emotional for me. You get close to the kids. You worry about them. You wonder, "Is the next guy going to take good care of these kids?"

Altogether, it turned out to be awesome being back in Glens Falls. I really enjoyed the American league. It was a lot like coaching junior because Adirondack had really young teams in those years. Some of the kids I was coaching had played with or against teams I'd coached in junior hockey. They were a bunch of young guys on their way up. They were very hungry. They worked hard.

We made the playoffs two years running, and in my third year we won the Calder Cup by beating Toronto's farm team in the finals. It was a unique final because the road team won every game. We won four games in St. John's, and they won three games in Glens Falls. That's the first time that's ever happened in all of pro sports. Three good years in Adirondack were capped off with the Calder Cup.

There's a big difference between being the better team and being the more talented team. The ditches along the road to the Stanley Cup are littered with more talented teams. Talent is only valuable if it is combined with a solid work ethic, strong character, passion, and all the other things that embody our sport. The Washington Capitals have probably been the most talented team in the NHL for about four years. Yet they have won only two playoffs rounds in that time.

By itself, talent does not breed success. Many people don't understand that, including several GMs I know. A lot of GMs over the years have put together the twenty most talented guys they could find, and here's a fact: those teams never win. It all comes back to chemistry. I've talked about that, and I can't think of a better word.

Good chemistry in the dressing room depends on a group of guys that love being together, who will compete hard every night, a group of guys who hate losing, who will do just about anything not to lose. When all that exists, you've got something special. You'll have a bunch of dedicated players who will go to their knees to block slap shots, guys who never quit, guys who finish checks all night long. You'll have guys who love to play hockey with each other and who have a blast together. Those are the kind of teams that win.

Every once in a while, you get a very talented team that plays like that. The Chicago Blackhawks are a good example. When Chicago won the Stanley Cup in 2010, they were one of the most talented teams in the NHL. They also had chemistry and passion, and they were able to put it all together to win the Stanley Cup. On the other side, Washington and San Jose have probably been the two teams with the most talent in the NHL from the mid-2000s on, but neither one has come close to winning the Stanley Cup.

Team building is the same whether you are coaching in the NHL or coaching ten-year-olds. We have a saying: "You cannot make a cake out of icing." If you have nothing but talent, the team is all icing. When you put a proper team together, you need the eggs, the flour, the milk, the vanilla – the works. As a general manager and as a coach, that's what you are trying to build – the whole cake. You need the talented guys, for sure, but you also need the tough guys, the characters, the nerds, and the funny guys, and you have to make that dressing room a fun place to be. Building a good team in junior hockey is exactly like building a good team in the NHL.

The endless search for the right chemistry is why there are so many trades in hockey. The typical NHL player has three or four teams on his resumé, maybe more. A guy who is a problem for one team might be the missing link for another team. Trades do change a team.

It's a shock to a team when you trade one of the guys. GMs do it a lot because they think it's a quick way out of trouble. Sometimes it is, but sometimes it's a killer, because the GM might make a mistake. He might trade a guy whose numbers aren't that great. On paper, the player doesn't look that important to the team. But maybe the GM doesn't understand what that guy means to the team in terms of chemistry – he underestimates the glue that player provides in the dressing room, the kind of motivator and the leader that guy is for the team. A trade wrecks a team as often as it helps a team.

Making trades used to be easy. You could trade a player at any time. You could even trade money, picking up salary from other teams. Trading is harder now, with the salary cap, which started in 2005 as part of the collective bargaining agreement. Each year since then, the NHL has established a salary cap and a salary floor for each team based on percentage of all hockey-related revenues. Now, if you trade a guy making four million, you have to bring a guy in who is making four million. Contracts are much more of a factor in trades than they used to be.

Typically, a coach will go in to see the GM after a couple of losses and say, "We have to get a little tougher on the back end. Our defence isn't tough enough." Or "We have got to get some quicker forwards up front. We're too slow onto the puck." Or "We have got to get some hard-core checkers who can fly." Those are the straightforward, honest conversations coaches have with general managers. That's why the relationship between a general manager and a coach is so important.

The GM might go to the coach and say he doesn't think Joey can hack it – he's not quick enough. And maybe Joey is one of the coach's favourite players, so that can be a tough conversation with the GM. It's good when the coach is loyal to his players, but sometimes a more objective set of eyes is able to see the situation more clearly. There are always disagreements between coaches and GMs, but that can be healthy and productive as long as they respect one another and understand how to work together. Those two guys should always be tweaking their team, talking about their team, and putting all their cards on the table, because nothing stays the same for very long.

The two have different agendas. It makes the GM look good if his team wins with the guys he drafted. The coach doesn't care where the players come from. He just wants to win. Maybe the GM has a kid he drafted and the coach isn't playing him. The GM will go in and ask the coach, "How come you aren't playing Joey? He was a first-round pick, one heck of a player." That conversation happens all the time.

In response, maybe the coach says he likes the Smith kid better. He admits the team didn't draft him. He was picked up on waivers. But the coach says, "I don't really care how we got him, I want him on the team." The coach is saying that the kid they just picked up on waivers is helping his team more than the kid the general manager drafted in the first round. That's been an age-old disagreement since the draft started. All the coach sees is a good player, but drafting is the general manager's job, and he's defending his decisions.

Scouts are very partial to the players they scouted who got drafted. They protect them all the time. A coach might not be high on some kid, but the scout loves the kid because he scouted him, helped get him drafted, and wants to see him succeed. Of course, it's also good for the scout if his kid does well. But the coach doesn't have any loyalty to those kids. He's just looking at his hockey environment, and maybe he feels that particular kid can't play for him. That can be a tough meeting, when the coach and a scout get together.

In 1992, when I was coaching the Los Angeles Kings, we signed Warren Rychel and Pat Conacher as free agents. They came to camp without contracts. I loved those two guys. I went into the general manager's office and told him I had to have Rychel and Conacher on my team. The GM said he had two other players already, they had signed contracts, and they could do the job. I said, "Rychel and Conacher are exactly the guys I'm looking for. They're hard-nosed guys, they're meat-and-potatoes guys, they're fun guys, and the rest of the team loves them. They play hard, they practise hard, and if I'm going to instill the right work ethic into the culture of this team, I've got to have guys like them."

Then the GM said we didn't have the money and that we already had two good guys signed. The two of us went back and forth and back and forth, and I finally persevered and got Rychel and Conacher signed. On the way to the Stanley Cup finals in

1992–93, they were two of our most valuable players. That is a typical example of what happens in the NHL between coaches and GMs. But the coach doesn't always win those battles.

Right after we won the Calder Cup, I got a call from the Los Angeles Kings. They had gotten permission from Detroit to talk to me about being their coach. It's strange to say, but the Kings' call didn't interest me much. I'd been looking forward to coaching the Detroit Red Wings. My assumption had been that coaching Adirondack meant I'd be moving up to the NHL at some point as part of the Detroit organization. I was flattered by L.A.'s call, but in truth, I was a little concerned that Detroit had given L.A. permission to call me.

I spoke with the people in L.A. on the phone a couple of times. They said they had been watching my team play the last three years. They had really focused on the Calder Cup win. They said they loved the way Adirondack played, and suggested we meet during the draft that year in Montreal. I was going to be there anyway, sitting at the Detroit table, so I agreed. L.A. set up a meeting with me the day before the draft started so we could get together face to face.

I met with L.A.'s GM, Nick Beverley, at the Queen Elizabeth Hotel in Montreal and talked for a couple of hours. It was a really good meeting, but still, I didn't really want the L.A. job. The whole Detroit scenario was in the back of my mind.

A few days later, I was driving home from the draft and I got a call in my car from Mr. Ilitch, the owner of the Detroit Red Wings. He said he knew I had been talking to L.A., and he wanted to tell me he didn't want me to go to Los Angeles to meet with the team's management. He said he knew what would happen if I went there: Bruce McNall, L.A.'s owner, would fall in love with me and do whatever it took to get me to go there. I told Mr. Ilitch that I didn't want to go to Los Angeles, that I wanted to stay in Adirondack and then coach the Detroit Red Wings. That had always been my goal.

He told me that when the current coach left Detroit, I would get the job. It was a great conversation, very uplifting. After I got off the phone with Mr. Ilitch, everything looked very rosy. I wasn't going to coach Los Angeles; I was going to be the next coach in Detroit, sooner or later. That was just fine with me, because it meant an even longer stay in Glens Falls. That phone call put everything on solid ground.

Everything Mr. Ilitch said came true. The next day, Nick Beverley called and said he wanted to bring me out to Los Angeles to meet with some other people in their front office. I said okay. Detroit also called and said they would like to bring me out to Detroit to be the assistant coach. I said I didn't want to be an assistant coach, but I would gladly stay in Adirondack until I could be the head coach in Detroit. They said they would rip up my current contract and make a much better arrangement for me to stay in Adirondack as head coach. So everything was good.

I flew out to Los Angeles and met with the brass. L.A. was intriguing because Wayne Gretzky was in their lineup. How many chances do you get to coach Wayne Gretzky? That was L.A.'s big selling point, and it was a strong one. I thanked them for their interest, said I was very flattered, but that Detroit had made me a great offer. I told them that Detroit had said I'd be the next coach of the Red Wings.

After that meeting, Bruce McNall took me aside. Bruce said, "Barry, you've been around the game a long time. How often do promises like Detroit's happen? All of a sudden, their coach starts winning and he's there for the next ten years. After that, some guy whose name we don't even know becomes the star of the month, and he becomes the next coach of Detroit. On the other hand, there's a good chance we'll be offering you the head coaching job tomorrow."

I flew home to Glens Falls with my brain buzzing. I told my wife, Cindy, I thought L.A. was going to make me an offer. Then I called Detroit and told them the same thing. They asked what it would take for me to stay. I said I wanted to be the head coach in Detroit. They said they had talked about that possibility and could not guarantee when that might happen.

About eight o'clock the next evening, I got a call from Los Angeles at the arena. They asked if I was close to a fax machine. I said I was. They said they were going to fax me an offer to be the head coach of the Los Angeles Kings. I went into my secretary's office and told her I was expecting a fax from the people in L.A. I asked her to bring it down to my office when it arrived and not to let anyone see it. A few minutes later, she appeared in my office with a few sheets of paper. When she put them on my desk, she looked at me, smiled, and said, "Bye."

She knew what I was making in Adirondack. When this offer came in, she just put it on my desk and said goodbye. It was that good an offer, a four-year contract, but I still didn't want to go. I called Detroit and told them what the offer was and they said again that they could not guarantee when or if I'd be the coach in Detroit.

I had to do some soul searching. I did the old pros–and–cons thing, you know: L.A., great long-term contract, good money, a chance to coach Gretzky; or, stay in Adirondack with no guarantee that I'd be the next coach in Detroit. I loved the Detroit organization, I loved living in Glens Falls, we had a great team in Adirondack – on and on it went, pro and con. I sat down with Cindy and we eventually agreed that this was too good an offer to pass up. I called Detroit and said I was taking the Los Angeles Kings' offer, then I called Los Angeles and accepted the job as their head coach.

It turned out to be a smart decision. Bryan Murray was Detroit's coach at the time. He was also the GM. The next coach to come in was Scotty Bowman, one of the greatest coaches ever in the NHL. So if I had stayed with the Detroit organization in Glens Falls, I never would have gotten to the Motor City.

11

Welcome to L.A. (@ 7.3 Richter)

I was born and raised in a town of nine hundred people in the middle of Canada. I had lived in big cities like Detroit and Toronto, but they aren't much when you compare them to Los Angeles. Now I'd be shifting gears from coaching an AHL team in Glens Falls, New York, a town of ten thousand, to travelling three thousand miles cross-country and coaching Wayne Gretzky in one of the highest-profile TV markets in the world. The whole idea was taking some time to get used to. First, I had to fly out to L.A. by myself and hold a press conference. Then we had to find a place to live and check out schools for our kids. This was all happening in June 1992. Training camp started in September. We had two months to get moved and settled. It was quite a summer for the Melrose family, no doubt about that.

My kids had been moved around a lot by then. Getting used to a new school was still tough for them, but as a result of our many moves, my kids met people pretty easily. So did Cindy. I was very fortunate that my family could relocate so well.

One of the first things I wanted to do was meet Wayne Gretzky. Following that first press conference, which went well, Bruce McNall took a few of us out for dinner. I had already arranged to meet Gretzky the next day before I flew back to Glens Falls. That night, I was at the Marriott Hotel at the Los Angeles airport. My room was on the twelfth floor. Around four in the morning, I woke up because the whole room was shaking. First, I thought it was a dream. The floor was swaying, I'm not kidding. I jumped out of bed and ran to the window. I looked down and saw the water in the swimming pool surging like water in a glass being tipped side to side. I found out later that going over to the window is one of the worst things you can do in an earthquake.

It was the Landers earthquake. It registered at 7.3 on the Richter Scale, the largest quake in the contiguous United States in forty years. It was unbelievable. My room shook for three or four minutes. That's a long time for your world to shake. The epicentre was in the town of Landers, 135 miles to the east in the high desert. Some welcome to L.A.! Once the earthquake stopped, aftershocks continued for several hours. That was the end of my sleep that night.

The next morning, I drove thirty minutes north on Interstate 5 to meet Gretzky. There was earthquake-related damage all along the highway. Buildings were collapsed, some of the roads were buckled, and houses with swimming pools had damage from water that had sloshed out. It was a crazy, shocking day.

I was meeting Gretzky at a hotel. He was fifteen minutes late because of earthquake damage. He arrived in a minivan with his wife and children. They were all piled into this van, which I thought was amusing – someone with his talent and star power looking like any guy from the neighbourhood, taking his family to the supermarket.

I knew all about Wayne because I had played against him in the WHA and NHL, but this was the first time I'd had a chance to meet and talk with him off the ice. I was very nervous. There I was, a rookie NHL coach about to meet with the greatest player in the game. He didn't know me from Adam, and here I was, taking over his team. It was a big meeting. I had to get this guy on my side. I'm a firm believer that you only have one chance to make a first impression. This was it.

Wayne is very soft-spoken. He's not shy, but he is very careful when he meets people. He's guarded – a man with his celebrity has to be – but he's very friendly. He wouldn't impress you with his physical self. He doesn't look like what you might expect a great athlete to look like. He's six feet tall and skinny, maybe 180 pounds soaking wet when he was playing. But there's something about him. When he walks into a room, you know immediately that he's special. Gretzky never needed a big physical presence. He always won with his head, not his body.

We went into the hotel and had a great talk. I told him one word would describe the way I wanted the Kings to play: speed. My whole game plan was about speed. We were going to attack offensively and defensively with speed, and the defence was going to join the rush. Teams who had to play us were going to have to play faster than they ever had in their lives. I told Wayne I believed the team could do everything at full speed, that we could play at a tempo other teams didn't like to play at.

We could force players to play faster than they liked to play, and force coaches to coach faster than they liked to coach. We could dictate how the game would be played. That's how all my teams had played. We had won the Memorial Cup and the Calder Cup, and now I wanted to win the Stanley Cup.

Gretzky loved it. He felt the game should be played that way, too. Edmonton, where Wayne played before L.A., played a fast game and had won four Stanley Cups that way. But I wanted to take it to an even higher level. It was a great meeting. I figured on talking with him for twenty minutes or so, and we were there for two hours. The time had flown by.

The only odd thing was that his family had been sitting in the minivan the whole time. We had been so involved that neither of us gave much thought to the time. Afterwards, I met Wayne's family – his wife, Janet, and the kids – and that was it. I flew back to Glens Falls after my first meeting with Wayne Gretzky in the aftermath of one of Los Angeles's biggest earthquakes.

My coaching debut in the NHL got off to a rough start. The second day of training camp, Gretzky complained of a sore back. He went off to see the doctors. Later that day, Nick Beverley, the GM, came in to tell me the doctors were saying Gretzky would be out for three or four months – if he ever played again. That news arrived on the second day of my first NHL training camp. It was surreal. I had come to L.A. to coach the greatest player in the world, and after two days, he was injured, unable to play. I had to completely rearrange the lineup, restructure my lines. At least he came back. Gretzky returned to the lineup in February after missing half the year.

Coaching in the NHL was different. Every level you coach, the players have unique problems. In junior, the kids have no money. They're young, they're homesick, they have school problems, girl problems, those sorts of things. When you get to the AHL, players are starting to make a decent salary, but agents become more of a factor. The AHL is a transition league. There are younger players trying to ascend to the NHL, and there are older players trying to get back to the NHL.

When you get to the NHL, you're dealing with guys with a lot of money. In the NHL, agents are an even bigger factor. And any NHL roster is made up of older players trying to stay in the NHL, younger guys trying to establish a name for themselves, and superstars. Each of those groups has its own set of problems.

The biggest difference in the NHL is the money involved. The more money involved in the equation, the tougher the athletes are to deal with.

Almost every NHL player knows that if it comes down to a battle with his coach, the player's going to win that battle. That's a big reason a lot of college coaches don't make a successful transition to the pros. College coaches have so much control over their players. They have leverage with players' scholarships and control over their playing time.

In the pros, it's just the opposite. Money talks, and the players have the money. If I had gotten into a battle with Gretzky, he would have won that battle. That's a no-brainer. As a professional coach, you have to make the guys want to play for you.

If they don't want to play for you, the front office is going to get rid of you. It's a tightrope walk.

There are two excellent recent examples of players winning those battles. Superstar Alex Ovechkin struggled in 2011, but it was Washington Capitals coach Bruce Boudreau who got fired that year. In Anaheim it wasn't Ryan Getzlaf or Corey Perry who got traded, it was coach Randy Carlyle who got the pink slip (Bruce Boudreau replaced him, as it happened). When a team is struggling, it's a lot easier to get rid of one guy, the coach, than a couple of players. Players and coaches all understand that.

Junior hockey is different. The young kids know the coach has the power. But even in the American Hockey League, the only power you have as a coach is when the players want to play for you, especially the stars. Coaches do it different ways. It can be by laying down a hard line, it can be by gaining respect, but you have to find a way that brings players onto your side. Lindy Ruff has been in Buffalo ten years, Barry Trotz has been in Nashville ten years. Both have very different styles, but each has found a way to make the players buy into his system.

I have a three-year rule. Most coaches are fired within three years because they can't keep coming up with new ways of grabbing players' attention. At the end of three years, the players have heard everything you've got to say, they know all your tricks, so they start tuning out your message. Unless you are turning your teams over and getting new guys in there, three years is the limit. Their attention span is wasted, and you've run out of creative new ways of motivating them.

What you have to realize as a coach is that the players control the dressing room. The coach spends little time in the dressing room compared with the players. That's why the captain is so important. I always chuckle at those teams that let the players choose the captain. The captain has to be the right hand of the coach. He has to be sending out the same message as the coach. The captain and the coach have to have a strong relationship. I had a great relationship with Luc Robitaille in L.A. when he sat in for Gretzky. And when Gretzky returned and took the seat again, I had a great relationship with him.

You can't have the coach come in and say something, and the minute he leaves have the captain saying he's an idiot. If that happens, you're done. The leaders control the dressing room, for good or bad.

The group is the thing. Peer pressure is what motivates a team, because everyone wants to be part of the group. Detroit is a great example. That group has had the same nucleus for a number of years. Stevie Yzerman was the leader for a long time. When Stevie left, Nicky Lidstrom took over. The Red Wings are a great group that plays hard every night. They are total professionals. The message is always the same: work ethic, work ethic, work ethic. You're expected to do things a certain way in Detroit, and it all comes from the leadership in the dressing room. It will be interesting to see who takes over that leadership mantle in Detroit now that Lidstrom has retired, and whether the next guy will be able to keep the team doing all those good, stable things they've been doing for years.

You don't get the guys wanting to play for you by being a nice guy, backing down, and just being a "yes" man. You have to prove to them that what you're doing will make them money, will bring them success. You have to make sense to these guys.

If you make sense to your average, normal players, they will follow you because they would be stupid not to.

Some guys will feel discriminated against if you bench them. They'll feel that you hate them, or that it's your fault that they are not playing well. That's usually the players' perspective. When they are not playing well, they blame it on the coach. The coach isn't handling them right, they're not being treated right, they're not being played with the right guys. Most athletes are really easy on themselves.

A player can quit on you. He can just stop working and trying. The reason it happens is he feels you have wronged him somehow. Most of it is his perception, but that doesn't matter because to him, his perception is the truth. If he feels he's been wronged, or that you aren't handling him fairly, or he thinks he's not included in your system, not in your plans, that's when a player will decide to quit on you. As a coach, you can try to get him back, but that will rarely happen. You only have two options when a player quits on you: fire him or trade him.

One way or the other, you have to get rid of a player who quits on you because he will become a cancer in your dressing room. You're not just worried about losing him, you're worried about losing your whole dressing room. Tommy McVie had a great line. He used to say, "I've got twenty players in the dressing room. Five guys love me. Five guys hate me. It's those ten guys in the middle I've got to worry about."

That's basically how it is. It's those ten guys in the middle who you've got to get on board. You've got to make sure those five guys who hate you don't poison the rest of the dressing room. But if a guy completely quits on you, then you have to get rid of him, or else the organization will get rid of you.

It helps to have been a player, because you've been there, you remember how you used to feel in certain situations, you understand what the guys are going through. By the time players get to the NHL, most of them will have families. The married guys will be worried if their children are sick, and will have all sorts of other family issues that affect their behaviour, their mood, the way they play. Some guys have marital problems. The coach has to be on top of all that stuff. You have to keep your finger on the pulse of the dressing room.

As a player, if I was benched I would be mad at the coach, for sure, but I was also pretty honest about my ability. I knew that I didn't have a lot of leeway. I had to be at my best all of the time to stay in the NHL.

One of the facts of dressing room dynamics is that the guys who are mad at the coach hang around together and feed off of one another. One of them will say, "We've got a shitty coach." And another will say, "That's for sure. He's a shitty coach." Three guys in the doghouse will be sitting in an area together, motherfucking the coach. Getting to know the dressing room as a player helped me as a coach. All the guys playing well will hang around together, too. Things like that are critical for coaches to know.

You've got make sure the players are with you. You do that by being successful, pushing the right buttons, patting the right guys on the back, kicking the right guys in the butt, knowing who is who. Coaches even know which guys shouldn't travel together. A coach has to be careful that he hasn't given two guys who are travelling together a dressing down on the same night. If you make that mistake, the two guys have time in the car to start motherfucking you. But if you have given one of them crap, and have praised the other one, then only one of them is motherfucking you. The other guy is disagreeing, saying you're a good coach. You have to get the travel combinations right. You have to be part psychologist, part psychiatrist, and part con man. There's a lot of stuff going on when you're working with twenty guys in a dressing room.

That's why, as a pro coach, it's really important to have a team of good guys, reasonable people with good characters. If you have bad guys, guys who are overly selfish, greedy, or deceitful, it's going to be tough to coach them whether they play for the NHL, the NBA, or the NFL. You've got to make sure you have character people in your organization.

An example of that is when I fought hard in Los Angeles to get Rychel and Conacher on my team. That was a very important battle I had with the GM. I needed those guys because they were highly motivated, dedicated players. I knew I could work with them. They turned out to be very important to our success. Luckily, I had a lot of good guys in L.A. Luc Robitaille stands out. He's a great guy, one of the favourite players I ever coached. I also had Dave Taylor and Jari Kurri, both good guys with strong characters, team players. Because of that core of upstanding athletes, we started the year off great.

Those guys were pros in the true sense of the word. They responded to how I coached, and they loved playing the way I asked them to play. Robitaille had his greatest year under me. I was blessed with a lot of good people on that team. I got rid of a few, but overall it was a very good group, a team that played very hard.

When Gretzky returned, he struggled. Many people think his back injury came from a hit by Gary Suter, who was playing for Calgary at the time. I think it was in the Canada Cup, when Suter hit him from behind into the boards. It was one of the worst hits Gretzky ever took.

He returned to the lineup in February, the hardest time of the year in hockey. The season is long, and the dog days are in February. Everyone is excited in October, with Christmas and New Year's coming. After that, February arrives. It's a tough month no matter what you are doing. On the ice, teams are tired mentally and physically. There's still a long way to go in the season. If a team is going to struggle, it will often happen in February.

When Gretzky came back, the team was playing badly. A back injury is tough to recover from. And he wasn't twenty-two anymore. It was the worst possible time for him to come back. We were struggling, and so was he.

The way you react to injuries in sports – and I'm sure Pittsburgh handled the Crosby injury this way – is you hope your star player comes back, but you prepare for the worst. One thing I did was make Luc Robitaille the captain when Gretz was gone, and Luc never had a better year. He set the record for left wing scoring, with sixty-three goals. He really responded to having the seat.

When Wayne came back, it was a bumpy ride. It was my first year in the NHL, and my first time handling a guy with Gretzky's talent. I hadn't been playing him a lot after he returned because it was hard for me to take ice time away from guys who were playing well. What turned everything around was a dinner meeting with Gretzky, Cap Raeder, owner Bruce McNall, and me one evening in Quebec City. The four of us sat in a quiet corner and talked it out. I said my piece about Gretz struggling, and he talked about how he felt. He suggested the team might be better off without him. The rest of us said that was ridiculous. Then he said, "Barry, I have to play more. If you want me to stay here, I've got to play more minutes. I'm not the type of guy who can play fifteen minutes a night."

A great player needs to be handled differently. It was a great lesson for me. Gretz was honest at that dinner. He said he knew he wasn't playing well, he knew he was hurting the team, but he said if he was going to stay with the team and be a help, he had to play more minutes. He said he had to have my confidence in him. At that moment, I understood. I figured that Gretz knew himself and his body, he knew what it took for him to get cranked up, and I agreed. I said, "Okay, we're gonna play the shit out of you. So get ready."

I wanted him to spend more than twenty minutes a game on the ice. You could see him respond. With each game, he got better, stronger, more confident. Each game, you could see him having more fun. He started doing all the great things he can do. It was amazing to see.

All great players need more minutes. A third- or fourth-line guy can be effective playing ten minutes a game, but the stars need to play a lot more. As I showed more confidence in Wayne, he had more confidence in himself and became the Gretzky of old. Once we got out of February, he took off. He was on fire.

We were one of best teams in the NHL the last fifteen games of the season. A lot of it stemmed from that dinner in Quebec.

I learned that when you are coaching a superstar, your job is to put him in situations where he can succeed. You have to give him plenty of ice time, because so much of what great players can do is instinctive. They do things by feel, by thinking ahead of the puck. There's no way a defenceman like me, who had to work his ass off just to stay in the NHL, can instinctively comprehend that. I had to be very analytical when I played. I had to know where to be at all times. I had to think out every move. I didn't have a lot of instinctual feelings about where to be and what to do.

A player who wasn't great has to understand that being great is different. Being great is special. When Gretzky used to tell me he had a feeling that he should go to a certain area of the ice in a given situation, or that he had a feeling such-and-such was going to happen as a play unfolded, I simply had to accept it. When I played, I had to have black-and-white evidence that some-thing was about to happen. As a coach, I had to learn that the great players think on a whole different plane.

I felt that my job when coaching a special player like Gretzky was to put him on the ice in situations where he was under pressure to succeed. Gretz was one of those guys who would show up when you needed him the most. I'd play him more in big games when we had to win, when we could close out a playoff series, or win the first game of a series. I'd use him more in important situations. I'd have him killing penalties more in the playoffs, for instance, or I'd send him in to make something happen if the game was tied at 0–0 in the third period. The bigger the game, the better he would be.

I'd always give him more chances to excel at those times because I knew he would. He was like a superhero. I felt it was my job as a coach to get him in the game when he could do the most. And he would do it for us. Maybe I would double-shift him on the power play of a critical game.

Vancouver would play Pavel Bure's line a lot. Bure was a Russian import who had back to back sixty-goal seasons with Vancouver. They called him the Russian Rocket because of his speed, his acceleration. He was a great end-to-end rusher. Instead of matching lines with Vancouver, I'd play Gretzky head to head against Bure, which would help neutralize Bure and give Wayne more ice time.

Gretz could handle the ice time, and he wanted it. When great players are on the bench, they are looking at you whenever you make a line change, even if they have just come off the ice. You know they want to be out there. Wayne would always be looking back at me to see if I'd call his name.

When you start a game, you have the matchups you want in your head. In L.A., I had defenceman Rob Blake, one of the great defencemen of the last twenty years. I wanted him on the ice against the other team's top forwards. Cap Raeder, my assistant coach, ran the defence. Cap knew the matchups I wanted. I ran the forwards. My job was to get the right guys on the ice in the right situations, giving us the best chance to succeed. If I saw a team's third- or fourth-set of defencemen going out, I would throw Gertzky's line out there right away.

But of course, shifts only last forty-five seconds to a minute. That's how long the average player can go full out without getting tired and being outplayed. Or a shift might last five seconds if a guy takes a shot off the ankle. Shift changes make matchups complicated. You have to plan ahead, be alert to everything going on.

It's very hard because it's happening so fast. The bench is chaotic. I laugh at the people who sit behind the bench thinking it's the best seat in the house. I'm standing, the assistant coaches are standing, the trainers are standing. A lot of players stand. If you want to see chaos at its best, watch the bench. You're getting the next line ready, people are yelling, and you're watching the opposing team's bench to see who they are putting out.

You have to be calm. There's a lot of stuff happening on that bench, a lot of things you're looking for. Late in the period, for example, you want to have two centremen on the ice for puck control. Getting that right is important. If you lose control of your emotions, the players lose control. If you're screaming like a banshee, the players will be screaming like banshees, and everyone will lose focus.

You can't be yelling at the referee every ten seconds, or the players will start yelling at the referee. If you stay calm, when you *do* yell at the referee, then maybe it will have some meaning. He'll say, "Wow, Melrose never yells at me. There might be something to what he is saying."

The bench looks complicated, and it is, but the guys have known the system from junior hockey on. They know their coach and what to expect at any given time. They know what to listen for. It's a dance, really, like a ballet, with guys coming in and going out. The bench is a great place. The chaos is wonderful.

Great players want to be on the ice when the game matters. Coaches get in trouble with great players when they start overmanaging their ice time. When you have a great player, you have a horse that wants to run. There's no sense keeping him in the barn. Great players want to determine the game. As a coach, if I lose a game, I want to lose it with my best players on the ice. I don't want to be sitting in the dressing room after the game, thinking that I had the wrong guys on the ice. If I lose the game with the right guys on the ice, I can live with that. I would feel I had done everything I could have done as a coach. But if I'm sitting in the dressing room after losing a game knowing I had the wrong guys on the ice, that's my fault as a coach. That's what I mean by using your great players properly.

Coaching in L.A. was different for other reasons. After almost every game, I'd go into my office and there would be Goldie Hawn and Kurt Russell drinking my beer. Their daughter Kate Hudson was often with them, but she wouldn't be drinking any beer – she was fifteen at the time. They were huge hockey fans, went to almost every game.

One night after a game, I found Robert Shapiro in my office. He was the high-powered L.A. attorney who defended O.J. Simpson. Shapiro was a huge hockey fan. I got him to sign a puck for me that I still have. He signed it, "To Barry – justice for all." I remember I said to him, "I know you can't tell me, but I have to ask: Was O.J. guilty?" He turned to me and gave me that great attorney sound bite: "Barry, everybody deserves the best possible defence they can get."

Sylvester Stallone was around all the time. The fact that he was so short surprised me. The thing that struck me about

Hollywood guys is that most of them are so short. In California, the women are tall and the men are short.

Stephen Spielberg came in one night. He had a big entourage with him, and they all crowded around Gretzky hoping for autographed sticks. Gretzky's stick is unique. He bought the stick company so he could get the sticks he wanted. His sticks have a special grip, shaft, and blade. Wayne used three sticks a game. The trainer marked them, so you know if you have an authentic Gretzky stick that was used in a game. He ended up signing six or seven sticks for Spielberg and his friends that night. It was surreal, watching one of the greatest film directors acting like a little kid around Wayne Gretzky. The stars are in awe of athletes. All of them were uncomfortable in the dressing room.

President Reagan and his wife, Nancy, attended a lot of games and would come to the dressing room afterwards. Nancy was sharp and did all the talking. The President didn't say much.

We had a celebrity game every year, and I coached one of the teams. I like entertainment. I watch a lot of TV and I know more or less what's going on in that world. But I walked into the dressing room to look at my lineup and saw a couple of names I didn't recognize. One was Matt LeBlanc. The other was Matthew Perry. Some guys from the TV crew were there, getting set up for coverage. I asked one of them about LeBlanc and Perry. He told me those guys were in this new show called *Friends*. He said no one thought it was going to last very long. LeBlanc played Joey on the show, while Perry was Chandler. The show lasted a while, as it turned out – ten years. Whenever I watch old *Friends* reruns, I think about that celebrity game.

———

In 1993, my first year with the Kings, we made the playoffs. We won our first game and kept going. It was unbelievable, a dream come true, especially beating two other Canadian teams, Vancouver and Calgary, to get to the conference finals against the Toronto Maple Leafs. We had an amazing series with them, winning it in game seven in Toronto.

After we won game three against Toronto at home, I'd been away for several days, so I grabbed Cindy and took her to dinner. We walked into a restaurant in Manhattan Beach, and I got a standing ovation. That was L.A. It was an unbelievable hockey town for those two playoff months.

Right after the morning skate the day of game six in L.A., Bruce McNall, the owner, came into my office. He looked upset. I could tell he had something on his mind. I figured he was worried about the game. We'd just lost game five in Toronto. So I told him no worries, we were going to win game six. He shook his head, said he wasn't worried about game six. He said what was making him crazy was that he had three hundred seats available for that night's game, and he'd had *five* hundred calls from Hollywood stars who wanted to come to the game. Only in L.A.

Toronto was equally crazed about the Leafs. It was great weather, so I always walked to the rink in Toronto with Cap Raeder. He insisted on walking behind me. He said he'd seen people looking at me, and he was convinced some nut was going to rush up and sucker punch me from behind. So he insisted on walking five paces back. It was nutty because we'd talk all the way to the Gardens, the two of us separated by five paces. Toronto had last won the Cup in 1967, and hadn't been close since. They thought 1993 was their year, having beaten Detroit to make the conference finals. Toronto was very cranked up about the Leafs that year.

An odd situation developed during our first game with Toronto. ESPN was covering the series, and they were pro–Los Angeles because of Gretzky. The Canadian Broadcasting Corporation was also covering the series, and they were pulling for the Leafs. An all-Canada Stanley Cup final between Montreal and Toronto would have given them huge ratings. We not only had teams from two different countries playing on the ice, we had a network from each country fighting one another.

Don Cherry, who covered hockey for the CBC at the time (and to this day), is an institution in Canada. With his clownish wardrobe and in-your-face delivery, Cherry just may be Canada's best-known person. He was going crazy over the Leafs. He was interviewing their players and coaches between periods and at every other possible opportunity. He was all over them. My guys got sick of it, and said they didn't want to do any more interviews with the CBC.

I told the CBC our guys were fed up, and that there would be no more interviews. I told them the decision had been mine because what was going on was too big a distraction for my team. The funny part was I had more Canadian players on the Kings than the Leafs had.

Cherry went crazy on the air that night. He started calling me everything under the sun. He was saying what a terrible player I had been when I was young, what a terrible coach I was, and that the Kings had no chance of winning because of me and my coaching.

Meanwhile, my parents had gone over to Wendel Clark's parents' house in Kelvington that night to watch the first game. Wendel and I had played hockey together since we were kids. As I've said, his dad had coached us and we were cousins. Now Wendel was playing for Toronto, and I was coaching the Kings. CBC picked up on this situation, and thought it was a great small-town human-interest story. So they sent a crew to Kelvington to shoot a piece about the two families with divided team loyalties watching the game together. Then Cherry came on between periods and started on me, ripping me up this way and that. It was brutal, ugly, and created such an awkward feeling in the Clarks' living room that my parents decided it would be best to leave. The CBC ended up without their human-interest story.

The Clarks picked a heck of a night to watch a game with my parents. Toronto hockey fans still talk about that game. It was a very physical game. In the first period, Doug Gilmour, one of Toronto's hot guys – he scored thirty-two goals that year and had 127 points – was carrying the puck at centre ice when Marty McSorley came up and drilled him. It was a hard, open-ice hit, and I didn't think it was a dirty hit. But Marty really nailed him – separated him from his helmet as I recall.

Then Wendel Clark came in and fought McSorley. It was a great fight – maybe the last great fight the playoffs have had. Those two went at it toe to toe. Maple Leaf Gardens went crazy, like it was the days of the Roman gladiators. Pat Burns, the Leafs' coach, was yelling stuff at me and gesturing. We were only thirty feet apart. In the old rinks like the Gardens, there was nothing between the two benches. Pat was a little chunky then. So I looked at him and inflated my cheeks, like a blowfish. He went really crazy after that.

That McSorley–Clark fight is a great example of why we can't take fighting out of our sport. It was an emotional moment, the right thing for Wendel and Marty to do. Marty had sent a message, and Wendel had to respond for Toronto.

I have no doubt in my mind that McSorley's hit on Gilmour and the fight that followed won us the series. It fired our guys up, and it let Toronto know we had come to play every night. We lost that game. But afterwards, I walked in the room and told our guys that McSorley had just won us the series.

Every game after that was a dogfight. In game six there was another moment they still discuss in Toronto. A lot of people think Gretzky got away with a high-stick on Gilmour that wasn't called. The referee, Kerry Fraser, still takes heat about it. But hockey is the fastest game in the world. Things happen in a split second. Fraser didn't see anything. Refs are taught that if they don't see it, they can't call it. If they see a guy cut, are they supposed to think someone must have cut him, and it must be the opposing team, so they'll give L.A. a penalty? I don't think so. Fraser didn't see anything, so how could he call it? I don't think it was a bad call because Fraser couldn't call what he didn't see.

I'm always amused listening to Leafs people talking about that non-call like it meant the series. Toronto had us 1–0, then 2–1. They had us 3–2, lost game six, then game seven was in their building and they still couldn't close the deal. And they are blaming Fraser? We have human refs and linesmen, not electronic machines. How many championships have been won by a missed call or a non-call? That's part of sports. The Leafs can't believe a non-call happened to them. It wasn't a mistake, it was divine destiny for the Los Angeles Kings to beat the Toronto Maple Leafs.

As the playoffs went on, we got stronger and started believing in ourselves more. Gretzky was the catalyst. But the whole team came together and played really great hockey. Tomas Sandstrom finished second to Gretzky in points in the playoffs. Luc Robitaille and Rob Blake played the best hockey of their lives.

Gretzky had been traded in 1988, and this was 1993, so he hadn't been in the finals for five years. It was fun being around a great player who loved what he was doing. The bigger the moment, the more he stood out. He always wanted to be on the ice in key moments, and he always wanted the puck. In game six, Robitaille made the great play to him in overtime and he scored the winning goal.

After game six in L.A., the Leafs and Kings landed in Toronto at about the same time. It happened that the two teams walked through the airport terminal together. The Leafs looked dead tired, beaten. They weren't used to the travel. The eastern teams didn't travel as much as we did. I remember looking at Cap and telling him those guys were physically dead. I talked with the team about it, told them we could get off to a good start and give Toronto something to worry about.

Gretz had been taking a lot of heat up until game five. It's not that he wasn't playing well; Toronto was doing a heck of a job against him. But after he got the winner in game six, he came out in flames for game seven, getting a hat trick. Whenever Toronto got close, Gretzky answered. He says it was his greatest game. The stage was set perfectly for him, being in Toronto, in game seven, five years removed from going to the finals. His dad, Walter, had been very ill but was at the game. All things came together. Wayne had said his goal was to take L.A. to the Stanley Cup finals, and that night, he was one game away from reaching his goal.

He responded to the media ripping him because Gretz responds to everything. He doesn't respond verbally. Some athletes will strike back in the press. Gretz will shrug his shoulders, keep his mouth shut, and let his actions do the talking. That's what he did in games six and seven.

After we won the series, the CBC came to the Kings and asked who wanted to talk about the win on the air. The players declined, so I went over to the CBC studios and talked about the win. But Don Cherry wasn't there. He wouldn't come on the set. Cherry and I are friends now, and I've done stuff with CBC, but at the time his attacks were a big deal in Canada, and a huge deal in little Kelvington.

Before we had time for it to sink in, we found ourselves one of the last two teams standing. The Kings had beaten Toronto and made the Stanley Cup final for the first time in the team's history. Off we went to play Montreal in the Forum.

It was a great finish to an unbelievable year, a magical year. There I was, walking around Montreal, thinking, "We're in the Stanley Cup finals against the greatest team in hockey, a part of the greatest tradition in sports." It was a great time in my life, but it didn't last long. We only managed to win one game. Montreal beat us 4–1 to take the Cup. But it was a thrill being there, that's for sure.

There's a saying in sports: "Losing hurts more than winning feels good." That is so true. Losing the Stanley Cup will stay with me for the rest of my life. If you win it, it's got to be a great feeling. You've got the Cup, the ring – but having the chance to win the Cup and not doing it is awful. So few people get a chance to win it. To get that close, overcome so much adversity, and come up short is the worst.

The day a parent or a close family member dies is probably the worst day of your life, but hockey has meant so much to me that I haven't had many worse days than when we lost the Stanley Cup. We had a very scary bus ride out of Montreal that night. The city was a madhouse. Fires were being set, like in Vancouver in 2011. Gangs rocked our bus, trying to tip it over. We told the driver to just keep going or we'd be in trouble. When I woke up the next day and the realization dawned on me that we'd lost . . . that was as bad a day as I've ever had.

I thought for sure I'd have another crack at the Stanley Cup. I'd won the Memorial Cup in 1988 with Medicine Hat, the Calder Cup in 1992 with Adirondack, and in 1993, there I was in the Stanley Cup finals. I thought winning was a part of me. I expected to win the Stanley Cup because I expected to win every year. That's what made me a good coach. But that Stanley Cup loss still haunts me, and it will for the rest of my life.

We won the first game in Montreal. We were winning the second game 2–1 with a minute and a half left in the game. Montreal had no chance. They hadn't had many shots; they weren't even in the game. Then Montreal called for a stick measurement on my defenceman Marty McSorley. They said the blade of his stick had too much curve. There is a limit to the amount of curve you can put on a stick blade. The NHL legislated that because pucks coming off a stick with pronounced curve will dip and slice, and, at one hundred miles an hour, be very dangerous for goalies to deal with.

They measured McSorley's stick and determined it was illegal. A penalty was called, Marty went to the box, and Montreal scored the tying goal on a power play in the last thirty seconds. Then they won it in overtime. Instead of it being 2–0 for us going back to L.A., it was tied at one. Without a doubt, if they hadn't called that stick measurement, we would have won the game.

Montreal's goalie, Patrick Roy, had had a really hot year. He won a phenomenal eleven overtime games that year. Three of the four games Montreal won were in overtime. But without a doubt, what turned the whole series around was the illegal-stick measurement on McSorley. Without that, I know we would have won the Stanley Cup. I have to live with that. Whenever people want to talk about that Stanley Cup series, they always want to talk about McSorley's stick, so it brings everything back.

It's like the ball going between Bill Buckner's legs in game six of the 1986 World Series. That play cost the Boston Red Sox the game, but the more important effect on the team of that odd play was its subsequent loss of game seven. The stick measurement had the same effect on the L.A. Kings. That game wasn't the deciding game of the Stanley Cup. But if we'd gone back to L.A. with a 2–0 lead, we would have had great momentum going home, and would have won the Stanley Cup. I know that in my heart.

I'll always believe Montreal had people in our dressing room measuring our sticks. Until the day I die, I'll believe that. I know that Jacques Demers, Montreal's coach at the time, has sworn to the heavens that no one from Montreal had been skulking around in our room. I like Jacques. I played for him in Cincinnati. I consider him a close friend. But he's got one part of the story and I've got the other part.

It was my job to check the sticks. I made that clear in TV interviews at the time: the bench was my responsibility. The illegal stick was my fault, but the sticks I always checked belonged to Robitaille and Alex Zhitnik. Those were the two guys I was wary of. I knew both of them had "third-period sticks" they used late in tight games. Those sticks had flatter blades just in case someone called for a measurement. I'd always check to make sure those guys had their third-period sticks in hand. I never once thought Marty's stick would be over. That's why I think Montreal had been in our dressing room.

I never fussed with Marty about it. Yeah, his stick gave us a bad penalty, but we wouldn't have even been in the Stanley Cup if not for McSorley. He had a great year and unbelievable playoffs against Toronto.

12

Face On

The next season, 1993–94, L.A. missed the playoffs. The following year, my third season, I got fired with eight games left in the season. We had a new owner coming in who wanted to distance the Kings from former owner Bruce McNall, who had been indicted for bribery, fraud, and a few other things. We'd had the lockout, and we'd missed the playoffs by only one point, but that was as good as a mile for the new owner, who wanted to put his stamp on the team, make some changes, make some trades. We'd had a very difficult year with injuries. I hate to say that, because I don't like excuses. A coach is supposed to win with the lineup he has. I know that. But Rob Blake was hurt, we had two goaltenders hurt, and I was playing six guys from the minors on defence.

There's no right way of firing people. I've been in this business a long time. I know there are a lot of wrong ways to fire people, but there's no right way. In my case, it happened after the morning skate. We were in Los Angeles, and we were going to play Edmonton that night. After the morning skate I got word that the general manager wanted to see me. I went upstairs and was told that I, and my assistant, Cap Raeder, had been fired.

The GM gave me the old business about how they wanted to go in a different direction and all that crap. I'm really not that hard on guys who have to fire people because, as I said, there really isn't any good way to do it. When I have sent people down, or had to cut or trade people, I have tried to be honest with them. I bring them into my office, look them in the eye, and tell them it was my call, that we were looking for a bigger guy, or maybe a tougher guy. I try to be honest with them, because that's how I would like to be handled. It's tough on both sides no matter how you do it, so why not be honest?

Cap and I got fired. It was difficult because I had my seven-year-old son at the rink that day. I had to bring him into the office and explain to him what just happened. He started crying. Then I had to call my wife and tell her, and ask her to come and get us in the truck because I had so much stuff to take home. Cindy arrived at the rink very upset. We loaded all my stuff into the truck. Just as Cindy was leaving, the Edmonton Oilers were walking in, and she started cheering for them in her loudest Honeybees voice, telling them to kick the Kings' asses that night. It was quite a scene.

All the players had left by the time I came back from the GM's office, but word travelled fast. A lot of them called me when they found out, and that meant a lot. But getting fired is just part of the game. If you accept all the great things about hockey, you've got to accept some of the tough stuff. Being fired is one of them. I've been sent down, I've been traded, I've spent the night in the dentist chair getting my jaw wired together, I've spent a month healing a dislocated shoulder. I've had some of the unpleasant stuff in hockey as well as the great moments. You just have to accept the whole package.

I had just gotten home to my house in El Segundo and was sitting outside in the sunshine when I got a call from ESPN. The man introduced himself as Mark Quesnel, senior vice-president for production. Mark said he was very sorry I had been fired, but he said the network had really enjoyed my interviews on TV when we went to the finals and the work I'd done for them the previous year, and they would love me to come work for them. I wasn't doing anything at the time except sitting in the sun, so I said, "Hell yeah!"

A day later, I went to San Jose and helped broadcast a game. From there I went to ESPN's headquarters in Bristol, Connecticut, and I've been working with ESPN ever since. Luckily, I didn't have too much time to be sad about getting fired, nor did I have to start looking for a new job.

My relationship with ESPN had begun during the Stanley Cup finals in '93. During the playoffs and the finals I was interviewed many times by ESPN. I was basically on TV every day for almost two months. When we missed the playoffs in 1994, ESPN asked if I would help cover the playoffs for them. They said they had enjoyed my work with them the previous year. They liked my TV presence. I thought it was going to be for two weeks, but everything went so well I was there for the whole playoffs.

I talked to some people at ESPN during that time, and they put into words what I already knew: eventually, I would get fired from my coaching job. It happens to everybody sooner or later in this business. They said if I wanted to get into TV down the road, doing playoff gigs was great training for me. So it was a win–win situation for me, plus I enjoyed doing it. I've always been a good talker, so broadcasting was a natural for me. It was fun, I liked the people involved, and mainly, it was a way to stay in hockey.

Making the transition to broadcasting wasn't easy. When you're doing an interview, you're just responding to the person conducting the interview. You don't have to worry about what your eyes are doing, or how much time you take to respond to the questions. When you become a broadcaster, you've got to worry about things like which camera is shooting you, plus you've got a director talking in your earpiece, telling you how much time you have, posing a question, or maybe suggesting a direction. "Wrap it up in ten seconds, Barry" – that sort of thing. You have to be quick. You have to have your homework done and be able to think on your feet, be clear, and keep your tongue from getting twisted.

You might have something really insightful to say, but you don't have enough time to spin it the way you want, so now you have to find a way to say it in less time. Either that, or speak faster. Getting on TV and making sense is not as easy as people might think.

Because the Kings were in a huge TV market, when I first started coaching in L.A. the Kings' management group came to me and suggested I spend time working with a woman who would polish my on–camera skills for the interviews I would be subjected to and the press conferences I'd have to host.

I'll always remember that the Kings' PR guy, Ricky Minch, stepped up and said, "Don't make Barry do that." Ricky said the reason people liked me on camera is that I wasn't polished. Minch said, "You can tell Barry really cares about what he says. He's passionate about it." He told them not to put me through anything that would change that. I will always be grateful to Ricky. I never did any work with that woman.

When I got to ESPN, the same thing happened. Some of the higher-ups wanted me working with on-camera coaches. Some of the production guys made the same observation as Ricky: "Don't make Barry work with those people, because we don't want him polished, we don't want him 'professional.' We want him earthy, the way he is. We don't want to change the way he talks. We don't want to change the way he says things. We don't want to take the grittiness out of the things he talks about." Twice, they threatened to send me to presenters' school, and twice people have told me not to do it. I know that not doing it was the right decision for me.

They can teach you some basic things that are good, but the risk is being changed into a cookie-cutter TV presenter. You see those people all the time. They are coached to speak and enunciate in a particular way, make all the right gestures at all the right times, but along the way they lose their spontaneous selves. I've always thanked Ricky Minch for helping me avoid that pitfall. Ricky didn't let them turn me into a robot.

I've made some mistakes on the air. Early on, it was simple things, like looking at the wrong camera. When you first go on the air, you are overly cautious. That hurts your presentation, but at first it's all about being safe and saying the right thing. In

1995, about three months after I joined ESPN, former L.A. Kings owner Bruce McNall was indicted. The producer asked me for an on-air comment. I looked into the camera and spoke from the heart, saying how much I liked Bruce. I got high marks. The guys at ESPN said that was the moment I turned the corner from coach to analyst.

I'm different from a lot of the guys at ESPN in that I don't use a teleprompter, or even notes. I tried the teleprompter, but reading the material changes the way I talk. I have a lot of respect for the guys who use it all the time and don't sound like they are reading. But I show up on the set with nothing. I watch games – that's where all my material comes from. I don't have a big book full of notes like most of the guys. If something has to be scripted, I read it over four or five times and then present it the way I talk. I'm lucky to have a good memory. If Alzheimer's doesn't pay me a visit, I'll be good.

I've said "shit" on the air twice. Both times, I broke the first rule of broadcasting: always assume you are on the air. The first time was with anchor John Buccigross. We were doing *NHL Tonight* at 2:30 a.m. I was beat after watching games all night. John was kidding around as usual, ragging on me about my hair, getting us both loose. I turned to him and said something about not having shitty-looking hair like him. Ohhh, man, I knew right away I had blown it. Our luck was that that show wasn't rebroadcast, and not many heard it at 2:30 a.m.

The next time was just a year or so ago. We were doing *First Take,* in the morning. They had just played a skin care commercial. To get a rise out of me, the anchor commented on how good my skin looked at fifty, and wondered what I used on it. I was being miked at the time, but I didn't think it was hooked up. So I told him, "Chicken shit," and went on to say how my dad told me that, in the old days, the farmers rubbed chicken shit into their skin to keep it moist. That went on the air, live. The next hour, the anchor had to apologize for me saying "chicken shit."

There was some concern that the players might not be so willing to talk with me once I was a broadcaster, but that never worried me. I'd been there and done it all – played, been traded, been sent down, coached, made the decisions – and I can empathize with every situation I run into. What gets players, coaches, and GMs mad is when people who have not been in their shoes sit up there in the booth and tell them how it should be done.

My credo has always been to criticize the act, not the player. So I might say this or that was a stupid play, but I'd never say the guy who did it is a stupid player. When I say a goal is soft, the goalie might take issue and say Melrose is an asshole, but he can't say Melrose doesn't know what he's talking about.

As a broadcaster, I've never made it personal. There's nothing personal about sports. You are sent down because you are playing badly, not because you are a bad guy. I think I'm a fair person. I also love the sport. That's what I hope comes across: how much I love hockey and how much it has meant in my life.

Everyone talks about my hair, but I've always had long hair. I've always enjoyed long hair. Growing up, I didn't have any nice clothes. I didn't have a suit. I had lots of jeans. I worked on a farm. My grandfather and my dad each had one suit for weddings and funerals. When I got into junior hockey, I got a suit. I couldn't afford many clothes, but I always enjoyed having suits when I could buy them. Because of my upbringing, I've gravitated toward stylish clothes. I guess you always want what you didn't have growing up. Those are my trademarks now, my suits and my hair.

I had been working at ESPN for twelve years before I got an offer to return to coaching. I think I'd probably been resigned to the idea that that phase of my career was over. I didn't think I wouldn't ever coach again. But I was very happy at ESPN. From the time I was sixteen years old, I'd made a living from hockey in one form or another, and my ESPN job had followed on the heels of playing and coaching. I wasn't exactly looking for coaching jobs, or putting out feelers to teams.

The fact is, once you've coached, you always have a soft spot for the job. I love coaching. I love being in the dressing room. If you are an athlete, competition is what you miss the most. There's really nothing quite like the nightly routine of getting your team ready and playing the game, win or lose. And there's nothing better in this life than that feeling at the end of the night when your team has played well and won. The recollection of that feeling never leaves you. Being an athlete means you are a competitive person. When you are done coaching, no longer can you quench that competitive fire with a win or a loss. Former coaches miss that, and you can bet they are always ready to talk if a team calls.

ESPN is populated with former coaches. Call out "Coach!" in the halls at ESPN and a dozen guys will stop and turn around. They all talk about coaching, and all of them tell stories. I've done *SportsCenter* where we had former – mostly fired – coaches from all the major sports right there in the studio: Mike Ditka (football), Dick Vitale (basketball), Bill Parcells (football), Bobby Valentine (baseball), Digger Phelps (basketball), Herm Edwards (football), Bobby Knight (basketball) . . . it's a long list. Every single one of them can be tempted by the right phone call. Bobby Valentine was. In the fall of 2011, not long after the World Series, the Boston Red Sox called him and asked him to manage the team. In a flash Bobby, at age sixty-two, was off to Boston.

I'd always felt that if a new owner acquired a hockey team and was looking around for a coach, and if he had seen how my teams played and liked what he saw, that's how I would get another coaching offer. That's exactly what happened in 2007. When the new owner took over in Tampa Bay, he'd watched video of the Kings playing when I was coaching them, and he decided that's how he wanted his team to play.

The details were that a buddy of mine, Mike Butters, who played for me in Adirondack, was also friends with Oren Koules, the entertainment industry executive who was part of a group that bought the Tampa Bay Lightning. Butters had helped broker that deal. He put Oren and me together. A former player, Oren Koules had been with six different Western Hockey League teams as a junior. He flew into the Hartford airport, where I met him. We went over to a Starbucks and talked. He told me he wanted me to coach his team. He said he loved the way my teams played in L.A., he wanted his team to play that way, and he sketched out a contract for me. When we left Starbucks, I was going to be the next coach of the Tampa Bay Lightning. Just like that.

ESPN knows how it works. They know their coaches still hanker to be coaching. The notion that simmers on the back burner of their minds that they could be going back at any minute is what makes former coaches good TV analysts: they really know the game, their heads are still very much in the game, and they keep in touch with everyone in their sport.

ESPN was great. They said go for it, and good luck. They told me I'd always have a home there. I left on great terms with ESPN, thinking it would be years before I saw them again – not months. They knew I still had the itch, so they said, "Great opportunity, good luck, we'll be watching."

My new job with Tampa Bay lasted fifteen games. I was done just before Thanksgiving. I couldn't get the team to play the way I wanted. It was a really crazy situation. The main problem was that the players were friends with the owners. When the players can go directly to the owners about team issues, that's not a healthy situation. You are trying to instill discipline, and the players are out having a beer with the owners after the game.

Having players friendly with owners is an unhealthy situation that upsets the chemistry in the dressing room. Maybe you aren't that friendly with the star who is having dinner regularly with the owner. Maybe you start to think he might be throwing you under the bus at those dinners.

Tampa Bay was an impossible scenario for a coach. The players knew it was a screwed-up situation, and *I* knew it was a screwed-up situation. The owners knew I wasn't going to change, and I knew *they* weren't going to change. After a short period of time, they decided I wasn't the type of guy they wanted to run their team. I think they consulted with the players. The players didn't really like the way I was doing things, either, so it was an easy thing for them to let me go.

Today's players are very powerful. When I coached the L.A. Kings in 1993, there was one millionaire on the team. In Tampa Bay in 2008, there was only one guy on the team who wasn't a millionaire.

Group ownership is also more difficult to deal with, for both coaches and players. Teams with single owners are better in so many ways. With a single owner, everyone knows where the cheques and the decisions come from, and where the buck stops. There is so much money involved now, so many tough decisions because of things like salary caps, that one voice is a lot more efficient than four or five voices. The most successful sports teams have single owners: Art Rooney of the Pittsburgh Steelers; Mike Ilitch of the Red Wings; Mario Lemieux of the Pittsburgh Penguins; Robert Kraft of the New England Patriots; the Steinbrenner family of the New York Yankees.

You can't have it both ways as a coach. You can't be a disciplinarian and a buddy. You can't be disciplining guys, trying to convince them to do what you want, and have them out socializing with the owner. My termination was the right call because it wasn't going to work and everyone could see that. Calling it quits early was probably the best thing for me, because I could get on with my life without a long interruption, and could pick up with ESPN where I left off.

My first assignment back at ESPN was the Winter Classic, the annual outdoor game held on January 1 since 2008. This is definitely the best idea the NHL has had since the work stop-page in 2005. You might recall the NHL lost an entire season back then, but the restructuring that occurred gave the league vibrant new life and led to great success. With the Winter Classic, they've hit another home run.

Every year, they come up with ways of making the Winter Classic new and different. In 2013, the Detroit Red Wings and Toronto Maple Leafs will play at Michigan Stadium – "The Big House" – in hopes of attracting the largest crowd ever at an NHL game. The Winter Classic isn't just one game, it's a great weekend with junior hockey, an alumni game, AHL games, companies vying to use the ice, and public skating. It's a hard ticket, a winter destination for a hockey fan.

I no longer have any desire to coach. The experience in Tampa made me realize that what I was doing was the right thing for me, at the right time. My approach to the game as a coach wasn't a match for the NHL anymore. For the first time, I had difficulty relating to the players and dealing with them. I've always been a coach who challenges people. The players are so powerful now that they are in control. If they don't want you, you're not going to be there.

I rubbed a lot of the guys in Tampa the wrong way. It didn't take long for me to sense that. I know I have to be able to challenge people in order for me to coach the way I do, and the guys at Tampa didn't want any part of it. They didn't like me or my message. It was an eye-opening experience for me.

That brief stay in Tampa Bay got rid of that nagging old desire to coach again for good. And that has made me a better TV commentator. Now I don't have to worry about what I say, because I'm not even subconsciously positioning myself for a job. I'm not worried about hurting the feelings of some GM who might be interviewing me someday. I'm unencumbered, just telling it like I see it, and that's a good feeling.

13

Changes

Fighting in the National Hockey League will be stopped, eventually. There's a generation of players coming up that will be ambivalent about the value of fighting, and the league will rule it out. It won't be for maybe ten years or so, but eventually fighting will be gone. Somebody will rise to power in the NHL who thinks that all the league needs to do is eliminate fighting for the sport to suddenly take off and be up there with football, with sky-high television ratings. It won't happen while I'm still working, but it will happen.

Ending fighting is a bad idea. For example, there was a game between the Pittsburgh Penguins and New York Rangers during the 2011–12 season — it was in December — and it was an outstanding hockey game, one of the best games of the year. There was fighting early in the game, but it was fighting for a reason. Fighting occurred because of the intensity of that game, because both teams were so aggressive, so competitive and cranked up. After the fighting cleared the air, the game turned into a pitched battle between two very talented teams, a great war of hitting and wonderful, thrilling plays.

The fighting caused a stoppage in play, cleaned the slate of old baggage, and served to focus the players' attention on the job at hand. After the fights, you could see both teams start to concentrate, dig deep and play at a very high level. The game was fast, the passing was crisp, the plays were remarkable, the shots were hard, the hitting ferocious. That game displayed hockey at its best. If hockey loses fighting, it loses an aspect of what can make a hockey game really special.

Fighting in hockey was in the news big time in 2011. That was a crazy year. I've never seen anything like it. Three young hockey players died in 2011, and all of them were "enforcers," as the media put it. Derek Boogaard, who had just signed a $6.5 million dollar contract with the New York Rangers, died in May. He was twenty-eight. Rick Rypien, a former Vancouver Canuck player, died in August. Rypien was twenty-seven. And Wade Belak, with Toronto, died a couple of weeks later. Belak was thirty-five. Suicide was suspected in both Rypien's and Belak's deaths.

Boogard was a partier. He had demons. He died from an overdose of prescription painkillers and alcohol. Rypien had a history of depression. But Belak caught everybody by surprise. Belak was a model citizen. He was making a transition. He was going to do TV for Nashville. He was a team favourite wherever he was and wherever he played. Belak's death stopped all of us.

For me, Belak's passing was a grim reminder of Marc Potvin's death in 2006. I had become part-owner of a hockey team in 2005, the Adirondack Frostbite. They belonged to the United

Hockey League, which was in business for about twenty years. My ESPN on-camera co-worker and friend, Steve Levy, and I bought part of the Frostbite just to keep a team in Glens Falls (the Adirondack Red Wings had moved to San Antonio in 2002). We never made any money — just the opposite — but it was fun. In fact, Levy told me it was the most fun he ever had losing money.

I'd gotten my old pal Marc Potvin to coach the team. Marc had played for me on the Adirondack Red Wings when we won the Calder Cup, and he had played for me in L.A. Marc was a character guy, a good player, a perennial leader wherever he happened to be.

Every year in Glens Falls, we have a hockey game on New Year's Eve, followed by a party to welcome in the new year. Marc was there, and seemed to be in great spirits. The team was winning. A few days later, the guys would be off on a road trip.

I was leaving for Florida to play some golf a week or so later, and got a call from Steve Levy around January 12. He told me Marc had been found dead in his hotel room in Kalamazoo, Michigan. He'd hanged himself. There was no note, no explanation.

I about fell on the floor when I got the news. It was a real shocker because Marc was such a leader, a motivator. Guys went to Marc to get strength. He'd seemed fine when I had last seen him less than two weeks before. He was in the midst of a divorce, but if everyone getting a divorce committed suicide, half the people in this country would be dead.

Marc doted on his two kids, he had no drinking problem, and he didn't use drugs to my knowledge. I remember thinking if this guy could commit suicide, then anyone could.

Marc was a good hockey player and, as with me, fighting was part of his game. Actually, he was more of an enforcer than I was. He fought his whole career. My initial reaction to those who would connect the deaths of Boogaard, Rypien, and Belak to the fact they were all fighters was that there is insufficient evidence to support that conclusion. My reasoning was, if fighting was a primary cause of their deaths, how come we haven't had more hockey fighters dying young over the years?

But when you add Marc Potvin to the mix, and also Bob Probert, a former fighter who died of a heart attack in 2010 at age forty-five, you've got five guys, all fighters, all dead – three from suicide, one from a heart attack, and one from drug/alcohol abuse. It's something that has to be looked at.

CTE (chronic traumatic encephalopathy), a degenerative disease found in athletes who play contact sports like hockey, football, and boxing, was found in Probert's brain. CTE was found in Boogard's brain as well. And autopsies that have been done on fighters from the old days have revealed CTE.

The fact is, Marc Potvin is one of those guys who made his living with his fists, and he ended up killing himself. I often wonder if I missed something with Marc. Was he reaching out to me and I didn't see it? Did he say things I didn't pick up on? He didn't seem depressed, but clinical depression is often impossible to see – I've learned that over the years.

As a fighter, I was never depressed. I've always been a glass half-full guy. If I found myself feeling low, I'd kick myself in the ass and go do something about it. I found fighting very hard. I wasn't a true enforcer like Potvin or Belak, but the possibility of having to fight was something I thought about before a game.

You always had a pretty good idea who you'd have to fight if it came to that, and that could get you thinking.

It wasn't the getting hurt that scared me about fighting. It was the embarrassment of losing a fight. That hurt a lot more. You can shake off a punch in the face. Punches and sticks in the face happen all the time in hockey. It's losing a fight in front of fifteen thousand screaming fans that is the scariest thing to a person who makes his living having to be a physical player. That's why, if a tough guy gets beat, you'll see him fight again right away. He must, because he can't stand that awful feeling of being beaten that's making his stomach churn while he's sitting on the bench.

The Dark Ages required teams to have guys on their roster who were there solely for fighting. All teams had to do it to survive. You didn't want your good players fighting those tough guys, so you had to have your own tough guys. In those days, you had guys on the bench who might as well have had signs around their necks that said, "In case of emergency, break glass." Their only job was to fight two or three times a game.

Boogaard was a holdover from those days. So was Belak, to a degree. He was a decent player, but Belak was on the team because of his fighting ability. Rypien was a good player. Coaching had refocused him on being a fighter to make it in the NHL. But neither Belak or Rypien were good enough to play today without having a fighting role.

Fighting is way down in the NHL. *Time* magazine ran a story in December 2011, with statistics to show that fighting is down 70 per cent since the 1987 season. Some teams in 2011–12 reported that fighting was down 40 per cent from the previous season. There's not even a fight per game anymore in the NHL (there was less than one fight per game in the 2011–12 season, according to the website hockeyfights.com).

The pure fighter is virtually extinct. Toronto just sent Colton Orr, a tough guy, to the minors after signing a big contract with him just two years ago. They couldn't find enough ice time for him. Pure fighters have become dinosaurs. In today's game, you can't just be a one-dimensional player who sits on the bench and fights when called upon. The guys left who fight also have to be able to play. I was a fighter, but I could also play hockey. I would have been able to play today because I was a good enough player. So was Marc Potvin. Today's game is more like the period from 1940 to 1970 – the pre–Dark Ages. There were no pure fighters back then, just tough guys who could not only stand up for themselves, but who had the skills to play the game.

Shawn Thornton from Boston is a great example of today's two-way player. Thornton's been on two Stanley Cup teams. He's a character guy, talented enough to play when the game's on the line. He doesn't take bad penalties. Thornton knows when to fight, and he can fight anybody, but he's good enough to play every shift, good enough to score on a penalty shot. Thornton is a perfect example of one of today's tough guys in the NHL.

Yes, there is still fighting, but it's very rare by comparison to twenty or thirty years ago, and that might be where the game ends up. In today's game, you can't give up a roster spot for a guy who can't play hockey. If fighting is not disallowed in the NHL within a few years, it will become even more rare. That's the way the game has reinvented itself.

But one of the things I loved about the old days is that cowards couldn't play hockey. When I was playing in the '70s and '80s, if a person challenged you to a fight, it never occurred to you to walk away, even if you were greatly outmatched. You stood up and were accounted for, even if you knew you'd get beat.

If a person went down on the ice and covered his head, we called it turtling. Doing that was one of the biggest taboos in the sport. If you turtled, you couldn't show your face around pro hockey – or even junior hockey – ever again. That stigma is gone now. You'll see a lot of players these days challenged to a fight and they just skate away. Or they will turtle. There's no embarrassment to it now. There's no stigma attached to it now. Players will goad a guy into taking a penalty, and then turtle on him when he drops his gloves. That's not a sin anymore. That's a huge cultural change in the sport within a short period of time.

The so-called instigator penalty, assessed on the guy who starts a fight, was aimed at players whose only job was to fight. It's become blurred of late, and not called very often, mainly because those specialists are gone. Getting an instigator penalty called on you requires severe provocation, like pulling the gloves off the guy you want to fight. If two guys have been going at each other tooth and nail for two periods, and they finally decide to fight, the referee sees that and doesn't single out an instigator. That's what the hockey fight is for: to blow off steam, clear the air, settle differences.

Every time someone gets hurt in a fight, there's an argument about it. Our culture has become more and more overprotective, more passive – you see it everywhere. Kids can't even play dodgeball in school now. There is a group that wants fighting in hockey banned, and every year its voice gets louder.

Once my generation is gone, you'll see fighting taken out of our sport. There will be fewer people like me who think it exists for a reason, that it's a worthy tradition, an integral part of our sport's history. There will be more and more who say it's Neanderthal, that it's holding the sport back. The pendulum is swinging in favour of pacifists who don't like fighting in our culture. Eventually, they will win the battle.

The hockey subculture reflects society. A lot of players like fighting, think it's exciting, know it's there for a reason. There are also a lot of players who don't fight, who've never fought, and who would like to see fighting gone from the professional game, as it is in the Olympics. Right now, probably 70 per cent of those playing accept fighting, and 30 per cent are against it. But those percentages will draw even as younger players come into the NHL.

Some people might say it's for the better. But I love the fact that your character, your bravery, used to be tested. I loved it that hockey players were the undisputed bravest athletes in the world. When you talk to athletes from the other major pro sports – football, basketball, baseball – they all marvel at how a hockey player will continue to play with injuries that would take them out of the game. All of them stand in awe of that. For a hockey player, being out there with a bunch of fresh stitches in his face is a badge of courage. Hockey players really want to be perceived as the toughest athletes in the world. While I think that is still the case, it's changing a little bit. Now you don't have to be brave to be a hitter.

The older guys can't abide that kind of behaviour. It annoys me too. The guys who played before me, without helmets, felt disdain for the guys in my era, without a doubt. You see that attitude in all sports, the old "he couldn't have played when I played" routine. That certainly exists in hockey. And it's true, to some extent. I don't think the guys that play now are as tough as the guys were when I played.

When I played junior hockey in the 1970s, I wore a helmet. I had always worn helmets, but not face masks. But from then on, all junior players had to wear half-face shields. When I entered the NHL in the 1970s, I didn't wear a helmet. The league made helmets mandatory in 1979 (players who had signed before June 1, 1979, were excepted). Visors will be next. There's been a big change within the last forty years.

Older players look at today's athletes as pampered and over-paid. They don't think they have the guts former players showed. They don't think the new guys love the game as much as they did. They don't see them carrying the flame like they did. They think they're letting the game change too much.

But here's the truth: today's game is better, without question. I consider myself very objective. I played. I coached. I'm a student of the game. I've always thought it was very important to maintain the game's standards so we can judge the different eras. But that has proved very difficult to do in most sports. Times change, people change, equipment changes, and the games inevitably advance.

I look around the NHL now and am amazed by what the modern players can do. We've got defencemen who are six foot nine, 260 pounds, with amazing reach. They can cover a huge amount of the ice. Some of the goaltenders are six-five, six-six, and can move like cats. Forwards are lightning fast. The pace of the game is amazing, and so are the plays that are made at that pace. When older players say these new guys couldn't have played when they played, they are nuts.

One of the biggest changes in today's game is that everyone blocks shots. The Dallas Stars initiated that in the early 1990s. Coach Ken Hitchcock made shot-blocking a defensive strategy, and the team bought into it. Players took pride in it. As a result, it was really hard to get a puck on goal against Dallas. Now every team in the NHL does it. Today, there are players blocking more than two hundred shots a year. Shot-blocking is now an official NHL statistic.

In the old days, blocking shots wasn't for everybody. The idea was that the guy in net was being paid a lot of money to stop the puck, so why were you getting in his way? Goalies used to get mad at you if you tried to block shots. You'd screen them or maybe deflect the puck past them. When I played, my job was to get the guy out of the way so the goalie could see the shot.

For the guys who did block shots, it was an art. The Boston Bruins in the Bobby Orr-days blocked a lot of shots. That was before helmets. Guys would throw their feet at the shot, and as a result, the puck would hit the lower half of their bodies. Now, players just drop in front of the shot and expect the equipment to save them. The old guys had to do it right because they didn't have great equipment. But in either case, getting in front of a shot is not for the faint of heart. Shot blockers have to be fearless. It helps that the pads are a lot more protective, but a slap shot has an uncanny way of finding your face if you get in front of it.

Shot blocking has resulted in more injuries, mainly broken fingers, hands, and feet. Many players now wear an outer plastic cover on their skates so that if they do take a puck off the shoe, it won't break their foot.

Shot blocking has been a big change in the style of play. It's a lot harder to get the puck to the net now than it was thirty years ago.

Another big change has been the influx of foreign players. In the '70s, Canada supplied virtually every NHL player. The whole world plays hockey now, and that influence has helped the game change for the better. I love the speed. I love what talented guys like Sidney Crosby, Evgeni Malkin, Jonathan Toews, and Patrick Kane can do with the puck. The athletes are bigger, stronger, faster, and generally better than they ever were, with better coaches and better training. When you compare the athletes of today to the athletes of the '70s, it's like night and day.

Thanks to having more money, players have their own nutritionists, their own trainers and physical fitness guys, their own psychologists. It's all scientific. Every little thing is taken into consideration now. Even travel has been studied. Doctors and psychologists figure out when players should travel, and how they should travel.

Players are told individually what to eat, and when to eat it. Now they know that eating a steak the day of the game is the worst thing you could do. When I played, everyone ate steak the day of the game. We thought red meat was what you had to have.

Sports medicine has advanced to the point where each athlete is treated individually, based on his physiology. Injury prevention is a priority of conditioning. Weight training programs incorporate the latest technology and theories. Players now work out after games, which is a whole new theory. Years ago, we worked out *before* the game. After the game, your workout was opening six beers. Now, as soon as the game is over, the guys have circuit training because the trainers have learned that the most productive workout happens when your muscles are tired, not when they're fresh. When injuries do occur, some of the advanced technology available to the doctors results in amazingly fast healing.

It's a twelve-months-a-year game now. At the end of the season, players take a couple of weeks off to unwind, then they get with their trainers and weight guys and start all over again. That's why it's hard for a championship team to repeat in the NHL: because if you win, you keep playing until the end of June. After the two-week break, you start working out again the middle of July. That leaves you six weeks until training camp begins in September.

The guys who miss the playoffs are out in April. After a two-week break, they start working out in mid-April. They have almost five months to get in shape. Five months versus six weeks. That's one of the reasons it's hard for a team to win consecutive Stanley Cups.

In my early days, training camp was for shedding summer fat. I was on the edge of the fat-to-fit change. When I first got to the NHL, the older guys showed up really out of shape. A lot of them had barely been on skates all summer. They used training camp to get in shape. One big trick they had was to put garbage bags on, like sweaters, under their gear. It made them sweat so much it was dangerous. Their bodies couldn't breathe. Plus, they were taking "piss pills" to get the liquid out of their bodies. We'd be out there for two hours, and often have two-a-day workouts. It's amazing they didn't pass out. Then, after practice, they'd go out and drink a dozen beers, defeating the whole purpose. Today, if you don't arrive at training camp totally fit, ready to scrimmage, you get blasted by the media as well as the coach.

All of today's equipment – skates, sticks, helmets, pads – is designed by engineers. In the old days, it used to be designed by former players who would come up with better ideas, like Joe Hall, the Hall of Famer who went to a bootmaker named Tackaberry with some innovative thoughts about skates. Goaltenders were always fiddling with ways to improve their equipment to better protect themselves.

The designs for lots of today's equipment are tested in wind tunnels – a good idea. Why not reduce drag when you are racing other players down the ice, when speed is essential? The sticks are not made of wood anymore; they are composite, with outstanding flexibility. Today's sticks fire pucks like guns fire bullets. Even the sharpening of the skates is scientific. In the last twenty years, many things about the game have advanced light years.

Equipment improves every day. Skates today are unreal. Compared to the skates I used, today's skates are from outer space. Hold one of the modern skates in your hands and you think it had to be built by aliens. They are so light! Skates are made from materials that don't absorb water, and they dry quickly. Today's skates cost between four hundred and six hundred dollars a pair.

The old equipment got soaking wet, and weight was a problem. Now, all the equipment is light. The dressing room used to stink with everything drying. Now the socks and sweaters breathe – even the underwear breathes. The guys today have specially made underwear that breathes and dries fast. We wore the same one-piece underwear our grandfathers wore to stay warm.

The composite sticks are wonderfully flexible. Everyone now can rocket the puck. But they cost a lot – between two and three hundred dollars each – and they break too easily. The selling point of the composite sticks was that they were supposed to last longer. That's not the case. Watch any NHL game and count the number of broken sticks from slashes, even slap shots.

When today's professional player takes to the ice, he's wearing two or three thousand dollars' worth of equipment.

I would love to see them make the goalkeeping equipment smaller. If you look in the rule book, the goalie is supposed to make the save, not the equipment. In the 1950s, goaltenders were five foot five, or five-six. Today's goalies are a foot taller. Those big guys fill the whole net. And they are well coached. They know all the angles. They don't catch the puck as much as those who went before, because they rely more on the equipment. Smaller equipment would still protect them, but it would make them work harder to stop shots.

To reduce injuries, lots of experimental work is going on that involves more flexible shoulder pad designs, and improvements like putting a softer cap on the elbow pad to reduce injuries caused by elbowing. The manufacturers are coming up with better helmets all the time. Also, in the interest of reducing injuries, the NHL is tweaking the rules every day. The league is very active in that area.

All those are good things, but people tend to forget this is a physical sport played at thirty miles an hour on a big sheet of ice with sticks, hard rubber pucks, and sharp blades. There are going to be hits, and there are going to be injuries. The idea is to limit as much damage as you can. But when you make the decision to play hockey, risk is implicit. You agree to that when you lace up your skates.

When I decided to play the game, I had to acknowledge that the risk of an injury was acceptable to me. You can't play the game and enjoy all the benefits from it, and then rip the game because you get hurt. You can't have it both ways. I think most players accept that premise.

But the press can't really understand it. They say the sport is too violent. People who want fighting out of the game can't understand it. People who want hitting out of the game, who want to make it into a non-contact sport where no one gets hurt, can't understand it. Those people also believe in Peter Pan.

Football suffers similar contradictions. Fans crave big hits. Then the players who come up with the big hits get fined or suspended. First we glorify the hit, then we disparage the hit. We can't have it both ways.

The nature of hits will continue to be legislated in the NHL. It will come down to eliminating hits to the head. Any hits above the shoulders will be off limits, no matter where the guy is – if he's bending down, or even kneeling, whatever, you just can not hit a player in the head. That's the only way of eliminating concussions.

For most of the 2011–12 season, we had the Penguins' star Sidney Crosby out of the lineup because of post-concussion syndrome suffered from a hit to the head. Boston's Marc Savard had been out more than a year for the same reason. Having your marquee players out of the lineup has a negative effect at the box office, so if nothing else, that should have an effect on making hits to the head intolerable.

The league will put a severe penalty on hits to the head. You have to put the onus on the hitter, not the guy with the puck. The hitter has to decide in a split second – and that shouldn't be a problem, because hockey is a game of split seconds – whether or not he can hit a man safely. If he can't, he has to let him go.

Other rule changes will be made to get more offence into the game. Studies show that fans like goals. Most rule changes are aimed at putting more offence into the game, and to make it faster, more exciting. Of course, whenever a rule is changed, the coach's job is to find ways to circumvent that rule and find ways for his team to give up fewer goals. It's a see-saw battle that keeps the game interesting for fans, players, and coaches alike.

Tradition raises its head regarding rule changes. If it were left up to the old guys, we'd still be playing a game in which hooking and holding were allowed, as well as grabbing-on and blocking – games where 1–0 was a big score. The NHL has somehow gotten around that resistance. What's helped the league is that the rule changes they have made have mostly worked. When you make a rule change, it's important that it work.

As for the future, I think there will be a team in Quebec City eventually. The Canadian teams are doing so well, the nation's economy is doing so well – Winnipeg has done so well – that Canada looks attractive to teams in the States that are struggling. There will be expansion, but not for a while.

One of my criticisms is that the NHL plays too many games. In the perfect professional hockey world, teams would play sixty games and schedule more time between games. If you played sixty games, each one would be more important because it would count more. The players wouldn't be as tired, and they would be more focused.

I'm sure players in other professional sports will be nodding their heads in agreement over playing fewer games per season. While that makes sense, it won't happen. Professional hockey, along with the other major sports, is attendance driven. In hockey, dropping twenty-two games from the schedule would mean eleven fewer home games for each team, and that's a lot of unsold tickets.

Hockey's eighty-two-game season is hard. It is *really* hard. If a team makes it all the way to the Stanley Cup finals, it could play eight exhibition games, eighty-two regular-season games, and as many as twenty-eight playoff games. That's a killer schedule. Players are lucky to be alive at the end of that long road, let alone still playing well. In January and February, you'll see some bad games because the teams are so tired. If you reduced the schedule, giving players more rest days, you would have a better product.

I'm 90 per cent in favour of everything the NHL is doing. Hockey is charging into the future with a new TV deal with NBC. It's wonderful that hockey is now a number-one sport on a major network. Hockey is the centrefold, the building block for NBC's Sports Network. It's a good marriage. I'm sure that, thirty years from now, today's players will be talking about how much tougher they were, how the sport was better and more demanding when they played. That's just the way of it. I can honestly say I think our game has progressed. I have a few reservations about the direction the game is taking, but that just might be my seniority speaking. Right now, hockey is in great shape.

The Best

A ll told, I was active in professional hockey for twenty years, and they were interesting, formative years when the sport went through some significant changes and development. Hockey wasn't exactly in its infancy when I started playing, but compared with the sophisticated aspects of today's game, it was both a simpler and less equitable time for players. Today, there are salary caps and other restrictions teams have to abide by. The players' association is a powerful watchdog, and the league office has evolved into a progressive, corporate entity, coming up with new rules and events to market the sport to a wider audience. All that is to the good. But when our sport was a bit less polished, still a touch on the wild side, it tended to produce stronger, and often more entertaining, characters. Here are some of the best guys I played with or encountered along the way.

Funniest

Mark LaForest: Mark was a goaltender, so right off the bat you know he's nuts. We played together for Adirondack. Mark has a unique spirit. Nothing came easily to him. He had to work his butt off to get to junior, and work his butt off again to get to the American Hockey League. He ended up playing with four different NHL teams.

Mark is a hard-working, beer-drinking, friendly guy. After a big night out, the next day at practice, no one would be working harder. Mark loved life, maybe a little too much. He was always the life of the party. He's a guy you love to go out with and listen to his stories. He always had a joke. He was also a smoker. In between periods, the rest of us would be trying to catch our breath. Mark had just stopped fifteen shots and he'd be sitting outside the dressing room on a couch, having a smoke.

One of the nicknames he got was "LT" because his hair was so long it came out of his mask and covered his name. The only two letters of his name you could read on his jersey were the L and the T. His other nickname was "Trees," as in forest.

One night, we were returning from a game. We must have won, because we'd all had a few beers on the bus, been laughing and joking and playing cards in the back. Around four in the morning, we arrived back at the rink. We got off the bus and Trees got ready to carry the equipment bags. In those days, rookies had to help the trainers carry the bags. So Trees says, "You know what, guys? I think I can carry all these bags at one time." It was like Paul Newman in the movie *Cool Hand Luke* saying he could eat fifty eggs. We said no way. He said,

"I'll bet you guys a hundred dollars that I can carry all twenty of these bags into the rink."

Equipment bags are big and heavy. Trees stood there, straight as a ramrod, and put his arms out. We started hooking the bags on him. We hung them around his neck, across his shoulders, and finally he held his arms up over his head so we could hang more bags on them. He looked like a Christmas tree full of bags. You couldn't even see his head. We got all twenty bags hooked on him, and he started walking. It was hilarious.

He was like a robot. He took one little step, then another, and another. All of us were half in the bag, laughing ourselves silly, watching Trees loaded up with twenty equipment bags and trying to walk. He went about fifteen feet, and that was it. He couldn't go any farther. He collapsed on the ground under this mound of bags. We were dying. You can't imagine how this guy looked with twenty bags hanging on him. That was Trees. You talk about one of those wonderful, nutty guys who made your dressing room fun, that was Mark LaForest.

Bill Derlago: I played with Billy in Toronto. He had immense talent. He's the guy who would wedge the beer can in the crack of his butt in the dressing room. That was one of those crazy things that got a laugh no matter how many times he did it. He played mostly in Toronto and scored thirty goals almost every year. He should have been a better player than he was, but he was satisfied with just being good. The guy could have been great. He looked a lot like Father Guido Sarducci from *Saturday Night Live,* so of course one of his nicknames was "Guido."

Bobby Hull: Bobby was a very funny guy. I played with him in Winnipeg. I was twenty-two or twenty-three, and it was the last year of Bobby's career, so he must have been around forty. Whenever we would go on the road, Bobby would take all of us young guys out to eat. We'd sit in awe of him, like church mice, and Bobby would tell us hilarious stories all night long. He was bigger than life, loud and funny. Everyone wanted to be around Bobby Hull.

He told one story about him and his brother Dennis being out on the town one night. An eighteen-year-old girl approached Bobby and told him he'd had a one-night stand with her mother eighteen years ago, and that made her his love child. Without missing a beat, Bobby took her hand and said, "Well, honey, I would like you to meet your uncle Dennis."

Toughest

Bob Probert: I played with Bob with Adirondack and Detroit. I've seen him fight everybody and anybody, and he never lost. He seemed to get stronger as the fight went on.

Fighting is a skill. Just like you have the best skater in the NHL, or the guy with the hardest shot, or the best playmaker, Bobby was the best fighter. He knew when to hold on. He knew how to switch hands. He never gave himself up for an open shot. And he knew when to fight.

Bob's hands never got hurt. I've never seen him cut badly. He could slip punches. He would take some punches early and they didn't seem to faze him. He was a great hockey player, too, and that matters. He was fearless. He stuck up for his teammates; he was always there for you. He always stepped up, no matter how he felt. He was a great kid – one of my favourite guys I ever played with. But without a doubt, from the 1970s into the 2000s, he was the best fighter to ever play in the NHL.

Joey Kocur: I grew up with Joey in Kelvington, and I played with Joey with Adirondack and Detroit. Bobby Probert was a better fighter and probably fought more, but Joey could hurt you. I can think of two guys – Jimmy Playfair and Brad Delgarno, known as the Bruise Brothers when they played for Detroit – whose careers ended with a punch from Joey. He had this big right hand that was basically destroyed. He had a blood infection in it one time. It was scarred terribly. That hand was so big it was like one of those Hulk fists they sell to kids.

Joey hurt people. Probert would cut you or give you a black eye. If you fought Joey, you'd end up with your nose, cheek, or sinuses busted. I think that's one of the reasons Joey didn't fight as much as other tough guys of his era. Guys were scared to fight him.

Dan Maloney: Danny was my favourite teammate in Toronto. For a few years in the '70s, Danny was considered the toughest guy in the NHL, the best fighter. He was a lot like Probert. He would stick up for you, and fight anybody.

Danny would get scary in a fight because he was so wired. He was crazy tight. He almost broke his stick just holding it. He had a real temper, and he'd lose it in a fight. When you have a guy who's six foot four, heavy set, and with really long arms, it's very tough to stand there and punch with him. When he went a little crazy during the fight, that was a bad combination. We would always wait until Dan's eyes stopped going around in circles before we would go out on the ice to settle him down.

As a fighter, you have to keep your cool. You know when you have to fight, you know why you're fighting, so you keep your mind clear and think about what you have to do and who you are fighting. Is he left-handed or right-handed? What are his strengths and weaknesses? You have to be in control. It's a lot like martial arts. Those guys are always in control of themselves. You have to find that spot in your mind where it's clear, and concentrate. That's what hockey fighters do. They're not fighting mad, or they shouldn't be. They're fighting because it's their job. They have to be in control of themselves to be good at it.

The guys who lose in a fight are the guys who don't fight very much. Guys who fight for a living are always in control. You never see them going crazy after a fight or pushing the referee. As a matter of fact, when tough guys fight, you'll see them actually pat each other after a fight. You will see them cuff each other on the head as they separate, as if to say "good one."

Dan Maloney was the exception, but he made it work.

Most Skilled

Borje Salming: I played with him Toronto. He played in the NHL during the toughest time, the Dark Ages. He was playing against the Flyers when the Flyers were the bullies. But Borje would walk into any building, anywhere, and not care who he was playing against. He was going to play the same way no matter who it was, and he was a tremendous player. He was one of the best skaters I ever saw. He was a great passer and a great competitor. He could do everything. I think he was one of the best defencemen who ever played our game.

In one game, Borje had his face stepped on by a skate. His face was almost cut in half. He got over two hundred stitches. It was one of the worst cuts I think any of us had ever seen. Borje put on a shield and came out and played the next game. That's how he was.

Borje was one of the first Swedes to come over. I'm sure that it was because of him the number of Nordic players coming to North America increased so rapidly. There was a strong prejudice in the league at the time against foreign players. All of us wondered why we should have foreigners over here playing when North Americans could do the job. That's why it was so important that the first foreign players were great. If they hadn't been, all the doubters would have said those guys weren't good enough or tough enough to play in the NHL. You have to remember that in 1967 there were twelve teams in the NHL, with players all supplied by Canada. Fifteen years later, there were twenty-one teams in the NHL teams supplied by the world, and the game is better for it. Since 2000, there have been thirty teams in the NHL.

For me, it took playing with the foreign guys to realize that they weren't only great players, they were good guys as well. Borje Salming was at the top of the list. Every night, he did something on the ice – made some amazing move, pass, shot, or play – that blew me away. Everyone who watched Borje play was really impressed. They figured if Borje was so great, there had to be other Swedes and foreign players of his calibre.

Bobby Hull: I used to watch Bobby in practice, and at forty, he was still the best skater on the ice. He still had a rocket of a shot. He was almost godlike to guys my age.

Bobby was known for his strength. He was a bull. There's a picture of him in an old issue of *Sports Illustrated* lifting hay bales. He's shirtless, showing off his massive shoulders and biceps. Farming provided a great workout. I did the same thing as Bobby, lifting hay bales, swinging an eight-pound mallet. My dad could stick a fork in a hay bale and lift it straight over his head and onto a rack. My grandfather could do the same thing. I was six foot two, 220 pounds, and strong, but I could never do that. And I couldn't swing the mallet as long as they could. Both my dad and grandfather were stronger than any athlete I ever played with.

Bobby Hull had big forearms and thick wrists. That's why he had such a strong shot. He was the greatest player in the game for a period of ten years. Bobby Hull was the face of hockey in the '60s and '70s.

He was like a Greek god, even at forty. I played a game with Bobby the night he turned forty. Afterwards, I was in the shower with him and Gary Smith, our goaltender. Gary was about three weeks younger than Bobby. He had the worst body in the NHL – one of those terrible, soft-looking, awful goaltender bodies. Bobby was standing there looking perfect. Smitty took a look at Bobby and said, "You know what, guys? If I have to look like that when I'm forty, I don't want to go there."

Adam Oates: I could easily pick Stevie Yzerman, but Stevie was only eighteen when we played together. He had his career ahead of him. I played with Adam on the Adirondack Red Wings. I'd rate Adam Oates up there with Wayne Gretzky and Mario Lemieux as one of the greatest passers who ever played the game. Oates played for Detroit, St. Louis, and Boston. He had tremendous vision. He was a very smart player, and fundamentally sound.

Oates could put the puck through a needle onto somebody's stick who was streaking to the net. Maybe there would be three guys on Oates, yet he would find an open man for a tap-in. Brett Hull says Adam Oates is the best passer he ever played with.

Smartest

Darryl Sittler: I played with Darryl in Toronto. He was a great student of the game. He could always see the big picture. He competed very hard, he could play both sides of the puck – defence and offence – and he made very few mistakes with the puck. If there was nothing there, he made the safe play instead of trying something crazy. He very rarely hurt his team. He was a very solid player because he was so smart about the game.

I used to watch Darryl play in the NHL when I was in junior hockey. He always played with passion, and with a smile on his face. When I met him, he was one of those guys who turned out even better than I expected. That's the amazing thing about my life that I reflect on from time to time. There I was, a kid in Saskatchewan with pictures of all these stars taped on my wall. Next thing I know, I'm meeting and playing with them:

Gordie Howe, Bobby Hull, Dave Keon, Darryl Sittler. It's crazy how my life developed.

Darryl had a great wife, Wendy, who died of cancer at a young age. She and I hit it off, and would have great fun when a bunch of us would go out for a few beers. She was always kidding around, giving me grief about something. One night, when she was distracted, I took out my teeth and slipped them into her beer. Everyone else saw me do it, and waited to see her reaction. She finished her beer, saw my teeth, and went crazy. I met her daughter at the Winter Classic game a year ago. She said Darryl had told her to ask me about the teeth in the beer story. She loved it.

Steve Yzerman: Even when he broke into the league at age eighteen, you could see that he was special. He had great poise, great maturity for his age. He's a quiet guy, humble, a guy who treated the older players with respect. And he never blamed anybody or anything for a bad night. He looked on the frail side, and he was when he entered the NHL. But he walked into tough buildings and played with courage. He was a great offensive player, a great passer.

Stevie was a tremendous two-way hockey player. He was like a sponge. He would watch other players and really learn from them. He worked hard in practice and was always prepared. He was very professional, even at that young age. He retired in 2006 and became GM of Tampa Bay in 2010.

Brad Park: Brad was a defenceman who could run power plays and dish pucks. He never panicked with the puck; he was patient.

On the point, he would get his shot through all the time; it never got blocked. When it looked like there was no possible path to the net, he would somehow thread it through a maze of arms, legs, sticks, skates, and pants and put it on goal. He would never have one of his passes intercepted. I played with him at the end of his career, when he wasn't as great a skater anymore, but he still played mistake-free hockey. Brad was a tremendous thinker, always a step ahead of the play. He knew where guys were going. He was a great player to be around if you were a young defenceman.

Brad always kept his composure. That's an important thing to do if you are a defenceman. If a forward makes a mistake, the attacker still has the defenceman to beat, then the goalie. But if a defenceman makes a mistake, the puck usually ends up getting on goal.

Park could cruise behind the net, pick up the puck, come out, and fake bouncing it off the wall. If the attacker bit on the fake, Brad would zip a pass up the middle. If the middle and the wall were both taken, he would skate the puck out. He did the right thing at the right time all the time. I loved watching Brad play. He played defence the way it was supposed to be played. If he hadn't been playing at the same time as Orr, he would have won six Norris Trophies.

Best Teammates

Robbie Ftorek: I met Robbie in Cincinnati. He's still one of my favourite guys. He's still coaching in the AHL. Robbie actually bought my wedding ring for me. I was young, and I was going to get married. I asked Robbie about wedding rings, and he asked me how much money I had. I told him. He said, "Give it to me." Robby knew a guy in the jewellery business. He got me an unbelievable deal on my wedding ring. Robbie Ftorek actually picked out my wedding ring. Cindy loved it, and still does.

Brad Park: I idolized Brad growing up because he was a defenceman. He's a great guy, and funny. He always had a story or a comeback. He was still a great player late in his career. He was great in the dressing room. He was always patting guys on the back. He never got mad at anybody or criticized anybody if they made a mistake. He was a calming influence on the ice and in the dressing room. And he was one of the best guys I've ever played with.

Ryan Walter: Walt and I lived together in junior. All my favourite teammates have similarities: all of them stick up for each other. They're always there to pat a guy on the back or pick him up if he is struggling. They are very sincere. If you needed anything, you could go to these guys. And they are great hockey players. Walt was a second-overall pick by the Washington Capitals. He had a great NHL career. Whenever I see Walt to this day, it's like we are sixteen years old all over again.

Paul Stewart: Paul came to Cincinnati my last year there. The WHA was really a tough league. Birmingham and Quebec were just like the Flyers, and we needed more muscle to keep up. So they brought in Paul. He was from Boston, with the typical

Boston accent, and he talked and acted tough. Usually, guys who talk and act tough aren't so tough. But we had a game with Quebec right away, and Paul went right over and challenged Wally Weir, one of the toughest guys in the WHA. They fought toe to toe. From that moment on, I gained a lot of respect for him. He stuck up for his teammates against everyone.

Paul told me his goal was to go into the Boston Garden and fight Al Secord, Terry O'Reilly, and Stan Jonathan. He only played twenty-one games for the Quebec Nordiques when they joined the NHL in 1979–80, but he used those games to attain his goal. He fought all three of those tough Bruins.

Paul is an NHL referee, a cancer survivor, and one of the bravest guys and best teammates I ever knew.

Pierre Roy: I played with Pierre in Cincinnati for a short time. He was French, and his English was very thin. This guy was one of the bravest I ever saw. He would fight anybody for you. And he wasn't a great fighter. It takes more courage to fight when you know you might lose than when you know you're going to win. But Pierre was unbelievable. He would fight anybody at any time to help a teammate out, or to help the team win. We became really good friends. I really loved the way he played, and I loved his passion for the sport. His broken English didn't matter. The way he played and conducted himself spoke volumes. If he had a point he wanted to get across, Pierre would stand up in front of the whole team and do the best he could. That took guts, and the guys heard him. I have always thought a lot of Pierre Roy.

Best I've Coached

Wayne Gretzky: Wayne could have been a huge problem because he was such a superstar. Superstars are virtually untouchable. They have amazing power in the dressing room and in the boardroom, so they can either be your biggest asset or your biggest problem. Wayne was the Kings' – and my – biggest asset. I think what I liked most about him was that he loved being at the rink. He loved practice. He loved being with his teammates. That's when he felt most at ease. That's when you could see what Wayne Gretzky was really like.

Wayne loved interacting with the team. He loved laughing, joking, telling stories, and having a beer – just being one of the guys. When he was with his teammates, he didn't have to be guarded, he didn't have to watch what he said. He could be himself. He loved that time, those two hours during practice, or before and after games, when he was with his teammates. That's when he didn't have to be the Wayne Gretzky everyone saw off the ice.

Wayne never abused his celebrity. I coached him for three years and he never once asked me if he could miss a practice for a commercial he was doing, or for any other reason. Not once. With all the stuff he had going on, all the endorsements and commercials, all the league obligations, and the team responsibilities, not once did he come into my office and ask to be excused, even from a morning skate. Practice would always come first for Wayne. He would set his schedule around practice time.

Luc Robitaille: I coached Luc in L.A. He either had a smile on his face or he was outright laughing. Luc was a guy who loved playing the game. He loved scoring. That made him happier than anything in the world. His brand of happiness was infectious. It was hard to be in a bad mood with Luc around, because he always seemed to be so up.

Luc had been the one-hundred-and-eightieth pick overall in the draft but went on to become a Hall of Fame player. Luc realized that he was one of the luckiest guys in the world, and every day he acted like he appreciated it.

Tony Granato: He was a really fiery guy, a great player who had three thirty-goal seasons when I was his coach in L.A. I used to battle with him. He would take a bad penalty, maybe he would slash somebody, and I would bring him in my office and I'd say, "Tony you can't do that." And he'd say, "Well, he whacked me!" And I'd say, "It doesn't matter. You can't do it back." We'd go back and forth. He always had his kids with him. At that time, they were three, two, and one. After we'd have these discussions, these three little kids would come running into my office and go right to my fridge. They'd go in there and get three Diet Cokes and sit on the couch, drinking them and looking at me. About twenty minutes later, Tony would poke his head in and say, "Hey, have you seen my kids?" Tony was fun to coach, a great guy.

Best Coaches

Dwight McMillan: Dwight was my first official coach. He was a great teacher and motivator. Dwight made me do things I never thought I could do, like fighting. When I first came to

Weyburn, I was a physical player. I'd had fights, but I didn't consider fighting part of my role. Dwight said, "You have to do this. This is going to be part of your game. You can't play unless you do this." He made me go out there and fight. It turned me into a more complete player, and taught me to stand up for myself.

Dwight could give you hell, really scream and holler at you, but five minutes later he'd be laughing and joking with you. That's one thing I picked up from Dwight. He could be like a marine drill sergeant at times. But as mad as he ever got at you, you never once thought it was personal. You knew he was doing it to make you a better player, a better person. And it did.

I thought he demanded more from me than any of the other players. I got more shit from him than anybody. I look back now and know it was because he saw more potential in me than he did in the other guys. He set a higher standard for me. And that made me a better player. He knew I could go on to the Western Hockey League and beyond, so he refused to accept mediocrity of any sort from me.

Bill Dineen: He was my coach in Adirondack. Bill coached in both the WHA and the NHL, and showed me that you don't have to be hated by your players in order to be a good coach. Everyone loved to play for Bill. He treated you like a man. He expected you to show up and be ready to practise and ready to play. He was an old veteran player who went on to coach.

Bill had seen it all and done it all. He started his professional hockey career in 1954, winning back-to-back Stanley Cups with the Red Wings. He was a tremendous storyteller. I used to love going out and having a beer with Bill and listening to his tales about Hall of Famers like Gordie Howe and Sid Abel. Howe is one of the greatest players of all time. He won four Stanley Cups with Detroit, six Hart Trophies as the NHL's most valuable player, and six Art Ross Trophies as the league's leading scorer. *The Hockey News* named Howe number three in its list of the greatest players of all time, behind Gretzky and Orr. Talk about a legend.

Sid Abel's playing career lasted from the late 1930s to the early 1950s. He coached for twenty years after that. He won three Stanley Cups with Detroit. Abel was also named one of the 100 greatest players by *The Hockey News*. Bill Dineen had great stories about those guys, and about all the people he had played with.

He would talk about Jack Adams, another Hall of Fame player who was coach and GM of Detroit for many years. Jack played in the 1920s. He's the only man in history to have his name on the Stanley Cup as player, coach, and GM.

Bill Dineen was a historian who knew about how the game used to be. As a student of the game myself, I loved his stories. I relish hockey's traditions. I loved what the game was like when I was watching it as a kid. Bill provided a clear look into hockey's past. He was probably the nicest man I've ever met in hockey.

Bill did things differently. Once, he was making his annual trip from Houston, where he was coaching, to Colorado, where he spent summers. He had his five boys with him. He stopped somewhere to buy fishing gear, and when he came out of the store there was a crowd around his car. He pushed in to find out what was going on, and saw his two oldest boys, eleven and twelve, having a big scrap in the back seat. They both had bloody lips and welts on their faces, and they were slugging away, pounding on each other. The younger boys were hunkered down in the front seat. Some guy in the group muttered he'd like to know whose kids they were so they could get the fight stopped. Bill Dineen said he'd take a walk down the street and see if he could find the father.

Floyd Smith: He coached me in Cincinnati before he joined Toronto as a scout. He is the reason I went to Toronto. He played me a lot and turned me into a solid defenceman. Floyd was another guy who had some great stories. He had been a forward who played for a bunch of different NHL teams in the 1950s and '60s, Toronto among them, my favourite team as a kid.

I used to bombard Floyd with questions about the Toronto Maple Leafs of that era. I'd ask him about guys like Dickie Duff, who played in the early '50s before I was born, or George Armstrong and Tim Horton, guys I'd watched play and admired. I loved hearing him tell me who the good guys were, who was the strongest, who was the biggest partier, or that so-and-so always played with a hangover.

If you watch hockey on TV, you'll get an impression of players that is often false. Everyone on TV looks good, says the right thing. When you get to know those guys, some are better than you thought, and some are disappointments. I was always interested in finding out what guys were really like, and Floyd had the answers.

Best Nickname

Two People: I was coaching in L.A., and we had a young guy come up from the minors. At practice one day, I was listening to players calling out to this guy: "Hey, Two People, dump it in," or "Two People, pass it!'" or "Two People, take the shot." I called Charlie Huddy over after practice and asked him how come they were calling this other guy Two People. Charlie said, "Because one person can't be that fuckin' stupid."

Appendix: Career Stats

Player Stats

Season	Team	Lge	REGULAR SEASON						PLAYOFFS				
			GP	G	A	Pts	PIM	+/-	GP	G	A	Pts	PIM
1973-74	Weyburn Red Wings	SJHL	Statistics Unavailable										
1974-75	Kamloops Chiefs	WCHL	70	6	18	24	95		6	1	1	2	21
1975-76	Kamloops Chiefs	WCHL	72	12	49	61	112		12	4	6	10	14
1976-77	Springfield Indians	AHL	23	0	3	3	17						
1976-77	Cincinnati Stingers	WHA	29	1	4	5	8		2	0	0	0	2
1977-78	Cincinnati Stingers	WHA	69	2	9	11	113						
1978-79	Cincinnati Stingers	WHA	80	2	14	16	222	0	3	0	1	1	8
1979-80	Winnipeg Jets	NHL	74	4	6	10	124	-41					
1980-81	Winnipeg Jets	NHL	18	1	1	2	40	-12					
1980-81	Toronto Maple Leafs	NHL	57	2	5	7	166	0	3	0	1	1	15
1981-82	Toronto Maple Leafs	NHL	64	1	5	6	186	-26					
1982-83	Toronto Maple Leafs	NHL	52	2	5	7	68	-16	4	0	1	1	23
1982-83	St. Catharines Saints	AHL	25	1	10	11	106						
1983-84	Adirondack Red Wings	AHL	16	2	1	3	37						
1983-84	Detroit Red Wings	NHL	21	0	1	1	74	0					
1984-85	Adirondack Red Wings	AHL	72	3	13	16	226						
1985-86	Adirondack Red Wings	AHL	57	4	4	8	204						
1985-86	Detroit Red Wings	NHL	14	0	0	0	70	-6					
1986-87	Adirondack Red Wings	AHL	55	4	9	13	170		11	1	2	3	107
	WHA Totals		178	5	27	32	343		5	0	1	1	10
	NHL Totals		300	10	23	33	728		7	0	2	2	38

Coaching Stats

Season	Team	Lge	Type	GP	W	L	T	OTL	Pct	Result
1987-88	Medicine Hat Tigers	WHL	Head	72	44	22	6		00.653	
1988-89	Seattle Thunderbirds	WHL	Head	72	33	35	4		00.486	
1989-90	Adirondack Red Wings	AHL	Head	80	42	27	11		00.594	Lost in round 1
1990-91	Adirondack Red Wings	AHL	Head	80	33	37	10		00.475	Lost in round 1
1991-92	Adirondack Red Wings	AHL	Head	80	40	36	4		00.525	Won Championship
1992-93	Los Angeles Kings	NHL	Head	84	39	35	10		00.524	Lost in Finals
1993-94	Los Angeles Kings	NHL	Head	84	27	45	12		00.393	Out of Playoffs
1994-95	Los Angeles Kings	NHL	Head	48	16	23	9		00.427	Out of Playoffs
2003-04	Adirondack IceHawks	UHL	Head	1	0	0	1		00.500	Out of Playoffs
2005-06	Adirondack Frostbite	UHL	Head	1	0	1	0		00.000	Lost in round 1
2008-09	Tampa Bay Lightning	NHL	Head	16	5	7	4		00.438	

Index